D0952500

Praise for *THE REMEMBERING PROCESS*

"I love this book. It presents a powerful new way to maximize the Law of Attraction and accelerate success in any area of your life. It is a mind-bending and time-bending technique that absolutely works. I am already using it in my own life and with all my students and coaching clients."

— **Jack Canfield,** *New York Times* best-selling
author of *The Success Principles* and co-creator
of the Chicken Soup for the Soul® series

"I've been in personal development for more decades than most people have been alive, and I have to say that my good friend Joe Vitale and his co-author Daniel Barrett have created a very effective process for living a life filled with enthusiasm and passion."

— **Bob Proctor,** international best-selling author
and featured teacher in *The Secret*

THE
REMEMBERING
PROCESS

ALSO BY DANIEL BARRETT

MUSIC

porterdavis (with porterdavis)
Live at Eddie's Attic (with porterdavis)
15 Hours Unraveling (with Mike Meadows)
Central Artery (solo)
Shadows (solo)

ALSO BY JOE VITALE

BOOKS

Adventures Within: Confessions of an Inner World Journalist
Attract Money Now
*The Attractor Factor: 5 Easy Steps for Creating Wealth
(or Anything Else) from the Inside Out*
At Zero: The Quest for Miracles Through Ho'oponopono
The Awakening Course: The Secret to Solving All Problems
Buying Trances: A New Psychology of Sales and Marketing
Expect Miracles
Faith
Hypnotic Writing: How to Seduce and Persuade Customers with Only Your Words
The Key: The Missing Secret to Attracting Whatever You Want
Life's Missing Instruction Manual: The Guidebook You Should Have Been Given at Birth
The Miracles Manual: The Secret Coaching Sessions
The Seven Lost Secrets of Success
*There's a Customer Born Every Minute: P.T. Barnum's Amazing 10 "Rings of Power"
for Creating Fame, Fortune, and a Business Empire Today—Guaranteed!*
*Zero Limits: The Secret Hawaiian System for Wealth,
Health, Peace & More* (with Ihaleakala Hew Len, Ph.D.)

AUDIO PROGRAMS

The Abundance Paradigm
The Awakening Course
*The Missing Secret: How to Use the Law of Attraction
to Easily Attract What You Want . . . Every Time*
The Power of Outrageous Marketing
The Secret to Attracting Money

MUSIC

Blue Healer (www.HealingMojoMusic.com)
Strut! (www.GetUpAndStrut.com)
Aligning to Zero (with Mathew Dixon) (www.AligningToZero.info)
The Healing Song (www.TheHealingSong.com)
Sun Will Rise (www.HealingRockMusic.com)
At Zero (with Mathew Dixon) (www.AtZeroMusic.com)

THE
REMEMBERING
PROCESS

A Surprising (and Fun) Breakthrough
New Way to Amazing Creativity

DANIEL BARRETT
AND JOE VITALE

HAY HOUSE, INC.
Carlsbad, California • New York City
London • Sydney • Johannesburg
Vancouver • Hong Kong • New Delhi

Published and distributed in the United States by: Hay House, Inc.: www .hayhouse.com® • *Published and distributed in Australia by:* Hay House Australia Pty. Ltd.: www.hayhouse.com.au • *Published and distributed in the United Kingdom by:* Hay House UK, Ltd.: www.hayhouse.co.uk • *Published and distributed in the Republic of South Africa by:* Hay House SA (Pty), Ltd.: www.hayhouse.co.za • *Distributed in Canada by:* Raincoast Books: www.raincoast.com • *Published in India by:* Hay House Publishers India: www.hayhouse.co.in

Cover design: Julie Davison • *Interior design:* Tricia Breidenthal

The lyric from the song "Thinking Amelia" in Chapter 5 was reprinted with permission by Deb Talan.

Library of Congress Cataloging-in-Publication Data

Barrett, Daniel, date.
 The remembering process : a surprising (and fun) breakthrough new way to amazing creativity / Daniel Barrett and Joe Vitale.
     pages cm
 Includes bibliographical references.
 ISBN 978-1-4019-4159-8 (hardcover : alk. paper) 1. Creative ability. 2. Memory. 3. Self-actualization (Psychology) I. Vitale, Joe, date. II. Title.
 BF408.B3476 2014
 153.3'5--dc23
                                    2013040293

Hardcover ISBN: 978-1-4019-4159-8

17 16 15 14   4 3 2 1
1st edition, April 2014

Printed in the United States of America

This book is dedicated to my future self.
I want to thank you for all you have taught
me. I want to thank you for your compassion,
encouragement, and enthusiasm as I struggled to
relax and allow you to be. I want to thank you for
taking such good care of the people I love and for
taking such good care of this earthly body. Oh,
and for maintaining the Ferrari. Try to keep
it running well while I catch up.
With love,
Dan, in the Newtonian "Now"

I dedicate this book to the future you,
who is looking at you now and advising you
on what to do next so that you can attract
the most prosperous, happy, and healthy
future, which, in actuality, already exists
right now. Enjoy the moment!
Love,
Joe (I could be anywhere)

CONTENTS

"Sometimes you realize you have to actually make the room inside in which the joy can dwell, not the other way around; sometimes you realize that thing you created . . . well, it already existed before you. At the end of the day, you allowed these things to be— just knowing this has its own incredibly joyful sound."

— Alexandra du Bois, composer, www.alexandradubois.com

FOREWORD

First, let me tell you how delighted I am that Joe and Daniel asked me to write this Foreword to *The Remembering Process*. I'm only a recent admirer of Daniel's work, but I've studied Joe's work for years and consider him one of the real geniuses of our field.

Since the publication of my book *The Big Leap* in 2009, I've been continually amazed to see that one chapter of the book accounts for 95 percent of the "fan mail" that comes in: the chapter on Einstein Time. Thirty years ago, when I first started talking to audiences about how to bend and shape time for manifestation, I got a lot of blank stares. Nowadays, however, I get a lot of excited head nods. I find it very encouraging to see with my own eyes that positive evolution is occurring.

In *The Remembering Process*, you will have a rare opportunity to make an utterly radical shift in your concept of time. Any vestiges of your old time paradigm will probably disappear by about page 10, and that's a very good thing. At this moment in history, we can definitely use all the positive paradigm shifts we can muster. Changing your time paradigm is a great place to start because it (literally) affects every minute of every day. Change your relationship with time, and you change your life.

Now, hasten on to turn the page and enter the unusual world of Daniel and Joe and *The Remembering Process*. It's a world where a great many things become possible that weren't before. If you're a keen student of the manifestation process, I predict that this small book will make an unexpectedly large positive impact on you.

— Gay Hendricks, Ph.D.
Best-selling author of *The Big Leap* and *Conscious Loving*
www.hendricks.com

☺ ☺ ☺

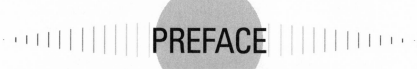

PREFACE

Remembering Your Future Past
by Joe Vitale

*"A musician can see past, present,
and future all at once."*

— Clifford A. Pickover, from *Time: A Traveler's Guide*

I met musician Daniel Barrett on Tuesday, May 9, 2006. I know the exact date because that's when Munrab Entertainment—which was basically me—hosted The World's First Canine Concert. The idea was to have a rock concert for dogs, played at pitches that only they could hear. The canine concert was performed by the Austin band porterdavis, and Daniel was their lead singer. The songs were silent to humans, and whenever the dogs did anything—scratched themselves, chased other dogs, ran in circles—we explained that they were expressing their appreciation of the music.

Of course, the whole thing was a publicity stunt to promote my book on P.T. Barnum, *There's a Customer Born Every Minute*. Even the company name gave a clue, as Munrab is "Barnum" spelled backward. It was all done in fun. Several news crews came, and Daniel and his band had a blast playing for the dogs. I never forgot the day or the wonderful gift that Daniel and his band had given me. They'd played the gig for free because they thought it was a fun, wacky idea and knew it was good for publicity.

I didn't see Daniel again for five years. He started e-mailing me in 2011, asking to have lunch. I was game to see him, but busy. He patiently waited (for months) until my schedule was free, and then we met.

It was a turning point for both of us.

Daniel was reaching out because he wanted some advice and encouragement about his life and business. After all, advice and encouragement is what I do: I'm a self-help author and coach who helps people reach and exceed their goals.

He told me over lunch that he was starting a program to enable people to record their first album. He called it the Rubicon Year, named after the expression "Crossing the Rubicon," a symbolic tip of the hat to the day Julius Caesar broke the law and led his troops across the Rubicon River in 49 B.C. Crossing that little river was Caesar's way of making his intentions clear: There was no turning back. The die was cast. In the same way, Daniel wanted to help people cross their own barriers and commit to their musical path. He said it was a complete training in music, playing, and recording; he'd develop artists from where they were to where they wanted to grow next.

What Daniel didn't know at the time was that *I* wanted to become a musician. I'd dabbled in music off and on my entire life, playing the harmonica in public after events, but not doing much else. Still, the desire burned bright inside me, and after putting it on my "bucket list," I had decided that 2011 was going to be the year I re-created myself as a musician. I'd written plays, poems, books, sales letters . . . just about anything you can imagine except songs. I wanted to write songs, but I had no idea how to get started.

That's when Daniel appeared.

I decided to share a private goal that I'd been carrying for years and told him of my idea to write my own music; perform my own songs; and do a one-man theatrical show called "Mr. Fire's Wonder Show: An Evening of Magic, Music, and Miracles." It's totally out of my comfort zone, but I wanted to do it anyway. Meeting Daniel again, after all these years, was becoming a defining moment.

We were both excited about finding a win-win for our meeting. I thought about signing on for Daniel's Rubicon Year but was hesitant. One of the things that sold me, though, was how he elevated my dream.

I told him that I wanted to perform my one-act show in Austin. He said, "This could be something you do in Vegas, and maybe promote with the tagline, 'What happens in Vegas transforms your life forever.'" I loved how he expanded my dream. Usually when I meet with people, it's me who expands their dreams. But Daniel expanded mine.

Not only did I sign up for his Rubicon Year, but I also hired him to produce my first album—which turned into two albums before the year was up. When I struggled to write my first song, though, he gave me another amazing gift: He taught me about a powerful tool called the Remembering Process.

He said, "It's easier to remember than to create."

It's easier to remember than to create.

He invited me to start trying to remember what my first song was all about: how it sounded, the lyrics, the melody, the chords. He wasn't asking me to create it; he was asking me to *remember* it.

I started to get high on this fun process. I told Dan it felt like an advanced form of *Nevillizing.* In my book *The Attractor Factor,* I invited readers to "Nevillize" a goal by pretending it had already happened. It's what spiritual teacher and philosopher Neville Goddard taught in the 1950s and '60s. It's a powerful way to implant a goal into your being.

But Dan's "remembering" process was as if you had gone way off into the future, way past the completion of the goal, and you were now trying to remember how you accomplished it.

The first time Dan taught me his method, I couldn't stop doing it. Our entire conversation was around, "I remember that my first song had this cool guitar lick in it."

I'd play the guitar lick. Then I'd stop and wonder what was next in the song.

Dan would say, "What do you remember being next?"

Obviously, there was no actual song in that moment; however, because I was trying to remember one from the future, it egged me on to be creative in a playful, curious, fun way.

And yes, I did write that first song. It has some catchy guitar licks and hypnotic lyrics. I found that I loved the process of creating by remembering, and told him he had to write a book about this process.

A few months later, Dan came to my home for my weekly preproduction session for my album called *Blue Healer.*

As he walked up the stairs into my recording-studio area, I congratulated him on something he hadn't done yet.

"Dan, it was great to see your book on the *New York Times* bestseller list. I felt proud to know that I was a part of the process. And I'm thrilled to see that you can still make time for our lessons with all the media requests and offers you're getting since your book hit the big time."

Dan stood at the top of my stairs and took in what I was saying. I was using his own process with him. He was letting it sink in. He knew he hadn't written his book yet, but he also knew that I was speaking from the future, reporting back to him what had happened.

"The reviews say your book is a breakthrough in creativity and has implications for quantum realities. Your millions of readers love your new process. And I loved seeing you on national television talking about it all!"

Naturally, Dan did finally write a book about his method. He had to because I saw it in his future and told him that I remembered it being a bestseller.

It's the book you're now holding in your hands. What I didn't see at the time is that I'd be the co-author. But I am, and I'm proud of it. This is a great gift to all of us.

When I explained the Remembering Process to singer Sarah Marie, I demonstrated it by saying, "I remember hearing that you received an advance of one million dollars for your next music CD."

Being a quick study, Sarah smiled and said, "Actually, it was for 1.2 million dollars."

I suggest you play with this.

Whatever your next goal or intention happens to be, imagine it's done and you're way past it in time. What you do next is remember the thrill of accomplishing it, and from there, you can play with remembering exactly how you brought it to life.

I remember how much you loved this process.

I remember that you bought our book when it came out, put the process into regular practice, and achieved your goals.

Remember?

INTRODUCTION

by Daniel Barrett

"It's like Schubert said: 'I don't make up my music; I remember it. I remember what I'm doing.' The only responsibility is to take care of it . . . make sure you're in good enough shape to deliver it, and make sure that you know what you're doing enough that you care about the moment you do it."

— Neil Young

I was writing a song called "Carter's Tune" in 1997. I remembered Emmylou Harris singing it, although the song had never been sung. I could see her onstage performing it with Lyle Lovett.

It was early in my music career, and that day I was running late for a job teaching preschool. The song came out in less than 30 minutes—whole and complete. I didn't write down a single word of it, yet I performed it in its entirety that night at a show.

It's still the easiest song I have to play and by far my most requested song. It has a special shine to it, even though I was an inexperienced songwriter at the time.

I call the method that produced this result the "Remembering Process," a game I invented when I was a music student in Boston in the 1990s as a way to deal with the "unrest" that is inherent in the creative process. Unrest is simply a form of inspiration before it has been put into some means of tangible expression. The unrest is like steam, whereas a finished project is like ice. Deepak Chopra writes in *The Way of the Wizard*: "The uncertainty you feel inside is the doorway to wisdom. Insecurity will always be with the quester—he continues to stumble but never falls."

When it comes to creating, my body and mind have always rejected "trying." I have tried to try. I think I've even tried to try to try. At best it produced inauthentic results, and, at worst, it just locked up my gears and led to creative depression. I needed a way to create without straining so hard.

The Remembering Process was an answer to that problem. It gave me a fun way to think differently about my music. I didn't have to try to create it anymore; I could just decide that it was already written and then imagine what it sounded like.

I became a professional musician and music teacher straight out of college, starting by busking (street performing) with a friend of mine in two subway stations: Porter Square and Davis Square in Boston, where we'd both gone to school. That's where our future band got its name: porterdavis. We added a third musician and moved our home base to Austin, Texas, in 2004. We play original

American roots and blues music, and won "Best Roots Rock" at the Austin Music Awards.

I've always had a great deal of respect and love for the musicians who've come before me, and I've tried to pay homage to them in the music we create. I've also paid attention to how they created their music. I read in an interview with Bob Dylan that during the 1960s and '70s, he "received" songs from the great universal source. He talked about them as though they were their own entities—whole, separate, and distinct from him or a belabored process of creation. He said, "I was just being swept by the wind, this way or that way."

Other great musicians have attested to similar experiences. I couldn't help but be curious about where these songs were coming from and inspired by the fact that, on occasion, I had moments when I was able to play the guitar in manners I hadn't consciously learned or thought before.

This notion didn't seem strange to me. It simply appeared as another way of knowing, spurred on by other synchronistic experiences I was having regularly, which couldn't be explained logically. It also fit in with other accounts I was reading at the time that caused me to question my views of the world. One book in particular had a huge impact on my thinking: *Autobiography of a Yogi* by Paramahansa Yogananda. That's a book that nearly everyone who embarks on a New Age path owns. You don't even buy it when you start on this quest; it's *issued* to you.

Yogananda discusses many important metaphysical concepts, including the astral plane and parallel realities. When I considered the ideas in this book, combined with musicians like Bob Dylan's experiences of "receiving" songs from a great universal source, I felt I needed to learn more.

All of these ideas were outside the realm of rational explanation, but they jogged something in me. I'd always felt there was more to the world than what we could see and touch, and now I was ready to go deeper. I wanted to know more about cosmic threads of inspiration, which started a lifelong study and path of balancing the common reality with these Divine, or inspired, planes of energy.

After stumbling into this paradigm, I began to experiment and birth songs in a new way—writing a few songs that felt entirely channeled. They came to me whole, with a feeling of peace and connectedness when they arrived, and well beyond my normal ability at that point in my music life.

I love music with a classic energy, so I often write by imagining the song as done and playing on the radio. I do believe that on some plane, all songs I'll ever write exist now—already written. I just have to remember them. Realizing that my best songs have been written in mere minutes strengthens this understanding. Other songs that take years don't have the same flow.

While the Remembering Process arose as an organic way of writing music that feels immediately familiar, it has a universal aspect. It can be used for creating anything: art, writing, music, relationships, career opportunities, and so on. It's a simple concept that can yield very powerful results, and my co-author, Joe Vitale, and I are going to illuminate it in six steps:

1. Relax

2. Agree with the Present Moment

3. Play, Trust, and Observe

4. Use Touchstones

We'll also tell you more about the "how" and "why" of it all—why the method works, how it relates to popular concepts like visualization and the Law of Attraction, and the ways in which it overrides the doubts and distractions that clutter your mind and stand in the way of creative breakthroughs. We share our clients' and friends' experiences using the Remembering Process, as well as many of our own personal stories of achieving success through "remembering." You'll see Joe's contributions throughout the chapters, as he "signs" each of his stories, adding his own insights and complementing the topic at hand. If you have even a kernel of belief in the idea that you can use the power of your mind to transform your future and manifest the things you want in your life, then you have all the foundation you need to use the Remembering Process successfully.

Joe and I used the process for creating his first album in record time. (Actually, he created five albums in two years, which is astonishing.) And, in fact, I used it to write this book. I began by writing letters, which I called "Remembering Letters." Rather than sitting down and trying to write a book, I sat down and tried to *remember* the book. I wrote not only about the words in each chapter, but also about the surrounding circumstances: how I felt while I was writing it, what scents I smelled and sounds I heard while writing, and what the reviewers said about it afterward.

In the following pages, you'll learn why it's helpful to write these things down. I've sprinkled bits and pieces throughout the book to let you "see" the process. You'll know the Remembering Letters by their look: sentences and passages in italics that start with "*I remember.*"

Once I began this book, I could feel the pull of "trying" to write, as well as the grace of "remembering" writing. I paused and breathed and put the process to work:

> *I remember this very moment: At my recording studio, drinking from a SmartWater bottle filled with tap water. The book Time: A Traveler's Guide to my left. Sheet music to Ray Charles's version of "Hey, Good Lookin'" on the floor. I distinctly remember this moment as a way station, a point in time, on my journey to the joyful and confident completion of this book. Yep. I remember I was a bit hungry, too, since I started to write as soon as I woke up. I remember that I was excited to start but unsure as to the shape and flow. I remember that this moment <u>had</u> to be part of the history of my imminent book.*

The energy of remembering brought with it sweet nostalgia, opening my breath. I allowed this moment to have a bit more vagueness and openness. I didn't hold the words with such control. I just let my memory wander back to the future. I wondered what I did next to help me get back on track with my writing. I wondered what I did to put myself into the right mood.

> *I remember that I watched a funny YouTube video to create even more good energy.*

This "memory" is a sensible, solid reminder to keep my energy light. The "remembering" has wisdom that "trying" does not. So that's what I did next: I didn't keep trying to force words to come out. I watched a funny YouTube video just like I "remembered" I did to get myself in the right mind-set to work more lightheartedly. Not all of the ideas we "remember" have to be deep and highfalutin. They just have to be helpful somewhere along the path.

Remembering the thing as done is akin to chess players seeing a win in their minds and working back from that.

Another great part of the Remembering Process is that there's no pressure involved to get it right. One of the beauties and skills required here is openness to the foggy nature of our memory. It allows for the possibility that something can be off by a bit. If you try to remember a happy holiday from your childhood, chances are that you may get some of the details mixed up: Maybe you're adding some relatives who weren't actually there that year, combining two holidays together, or misquoting who said what—but the overall feel is right. It's still your memory, imperfect though it may be, and you don't have to feel pressured to recall it exactly as it happened moment for moment. Really, who *can* remember that much? Our brains aren't designed to store every event in detail like a computer's hard drive. There's just not enough room in there—we'd have no space left to create new memories if we tried too hard to retain all the details of the old ones.

That's a freeing part of the process. When you put it into practice, you can allow for a little misinterpretation, creative license, and forgetfulness. If I try to write this perfectly, I notice I feel stifled and scared that I might say the wrong thing, but if I try to remember the wonderful version that is already out there in time and space to the best of my ability, a flow begins.

This process turns work into play, try into do, and when into now.

Albert Einstein said, "Your imagination is your preview of life's coming attractions." That's what this process is all about: harnessing the power of your imagination to create positive results. So let's figure out how to start doing that!

WHAT IT'S ALL ABOUT

"I am composing like a god, as if it simply had to be done as it has been done."
—Franz Schubert

The Remembering Process is about creating, having access to your own creativity, and eliminating struggle. Anyone who consciously creates material of any kind on a professional level—such as music, film, plays, poetry, books, or software—will tell you that the hardest part is to get out of your own way and stop trying so hard.

Lord Byron wrote, "The power of Thought—the magic of the Mind!"

I doubt Byron knew about "remembering," but he certainly knew about creating. When I was wrestling with how to write my first songs, I remembered that songs are poems. That thought freed me to write poetry rather than lyrics. I then

1

wondered what theme I wanted to project through music. I didn't know.

So I pretended that I was Lord Byron. I mentally allowed my mind to remember that I had already completed my poem-song in some future world. That meant I just had to tune in to it, like finding a radio station.

I let my mind get magical, and suddenly I was writing the line: "Two faces staring at me," which became the beginning of the song I now call "The Choice." I didn't worry about what the song meant; instead, I allowed the Byron in me to recall the song.

Now that it's recorded on the album *Strut!*, you can decide what it means.

— Joe

The Remembering Process arises out of a technique that I use to compose music. I "remember" the songs. I hear them coming out of the speakers. I see them performed in front of a live audience. I remember aspects of them before they exist in time and space.

However, there is another form of using your creativity and that is in the realm of creating your life—so you don't have to be an artist to use this process or benefit by it. Do you want to create a work of art? Do you want to create better health or more loving relationships? Do you want to create a new business? Whether you're producing results for your life on a personal level or a physical product, the Remembering Process can support you.

I remember that the process really helped me re-member a few keys to my dreams.

I remember that the Remembering Letters began a series of productive output for me. I remember that I smoked cigars instead of cigarettes, even when I craved the latter—a lesser of evils.

I remember a new wave of healthy choices—and if not healthy, healthier. I remember that incense, scented candles, and Palo Santo wood were fragrant aids to the process.

The Remembering Process works in harmony with the principle of the Law of Attraction, a metaphysical concept named by New Thought writer William W. Atkinson in 1906. Many philosophers through the years described the power of positive thought, including Napoleon Hill, but it hit the mainstream media in a big way in 2006 with the arrival of *The Secret*—the movie and then the book. In essence, it means that you manifest what you think. You attract things into your life based on what you think about and focus on. So if you think, "I can't afford that car," you won't. But if you envision yourself driving that car, and you spend time thinking about how you already own it, the Universe will rearrange itself to make sure that you do, in fact, wind up owning it. It wants your reality to match your perception. It works not only with tangible objects, but also with desires, such as good health, happiness, prosperity, a new relationship, a sports winning streak, and so on.

The Remembering Process teaches us to think as if we're already past achieving those things we want and reporting back from a point even further into the future.

When you do it, you create a space—a type of detachment—toward the thing you want to accomplish.

· ᛁ ᛁ ᛁ ᛁ ᛁ ᛁ THE REMEMBERING PROCESS ᛁ ᛁ ᛁ ᛁ ᛁ · ·

When something feels as though it has already happened, and has that foggy air of a memory, the ego can't reach it in the same way or figure out how to prevent it. When you "want" something, your brain can ruminate on a hundred ways of foiling your plan—*I'm not good enough, I'm not ready, I don't deserve it, I can't, I shouldn't, Other priorities should come first, I'm tired, I'll never have enough time, I'm not that lucky*—but when you're remembering it, it can't be prevented! You've told your ego that it has already been scripted and there's nothing standing in your way, so it might as well just accept it and get moving on it. *I have already had a successful exhibition of my photography* tells your ego that it can no longer make you question whether you'll ever be good enough. It reminds you that you need to make the time for what you love because something great is about to happen and you need to prepare for it.

It's like a cheat code for the soul, the brain, or both.

Judo champion Kayla Harrison used this practice when she trained for the 2012 Olympics. Instead of "wanting" to win, she remembered winning. Every morning and night, she remembered the future—the day in London when she awoke, went to weigh in, had breakfast, warmed up, waited in the holding area, then won each of her judo matches, and finally stood atop the podium accepting her gold medal.

When the morning actually came, she says she was surprisingly calm. All the other athletes around her seemed to be buzzing with nervous energy, but she didn't feel nervous at all. Kayla had successfully tricked her brain into thinking that her memory had already happened—that she had already won the Olympic medal and now just had to go through the steps to claim what was rightfully hers.

And that's just what she did. She took home the very first Olympic gold medal for any American, male or female, in judo. As she stood atop that podium with the "Star-Spangled Banner" sounding out across the stadium, she burst into tears. "It was just how I remembered it," she says.

> I'm a fan of spiritual teacher Neville Goddard. I've written about him a lot, especially in my book *The Attractor Factor*. I even republished his very first book, *At Your Command*. His method was to advise people to imagine that they *already had* whatever they wanted. If you want to have a certain job, imagine you are already working there. If you want a particular relationship, imagine you already have it. The more you can imagine your desire as a finished end result, the more you are "Nevillizing" your goal. Neville said (in *At Your Command*):
>
>> If you are dissatisfied with your present expression in life, the only way to change it is to take your attention away from that which seems so real to you and rise in consciousness to that which you desire to be. You cannot serve two masters; therefore, to take your attention from one state of consciousness and place it upon another is to die to one and live to the other.
>
> The Remembering Process goes beyond what Neville taught. Remembering means you go *past* the event of having what you want, and turn around and look at it *from the future*. Clearly you can't see the end result if it hasn't happened yet. So remembering lets you know that it *did* happen. How else could you remember it?

I still love Neville and his method. It beats most imagery techniques, as it adds the feeling aspect of joy and the confidence that your reality is now, well, real. And, as it turns out, Neville talked about a form of "remembering" in 1968. He used it as an imagery method, but the idea was the same: simply remember what you want to experience.

In a sense, you assume your new reality by assuming you already have it. As Neville wrote in some of the signed books I own by him: "Assumption hardens into fact." Assume you already have the thing you wish to have or be, and your assumption creates a new reality.

Neville also said, "The best way to do this is to concentrate your attention upon the idea of identifying yourself with your ideal. Assume you are already that which you seek and your assumption, though false, if sustained, will harden into fact."

Remembering builds on Nevillizing.

You not only get to do the Neville thing, but you also get to remember that you did it, which makes it even more powerful.

— Joe

Remembering is an *allowing* mechanism.

My true passion for the Remembering Process lies in the magical or metaphysical side of it. Think of this as a tool—a bridge across time and dimension—a way to call something into being that wasn't there before. Remembering truly acknowledges that these ideas already exist in their wholeness somewhere in the time and space continuum.

When the technique has been refined and there is mental and physical clarity, there is a place where the muses and the metaphysical winds can start blowing in our sails. And there are lots of ways to help create that—this is just one more. Living the life you dream is your opportunity to create heaven on earth. Take it easy, but take it. It doesn't have to be so hard. Just use your imagination to remember, and create ease and love.

Understanding Time: Newton and Einstein

Richard Branson, one of the world's wealthiest men, has created close to 400 companies. His motto is, "Anything is possible." And it's true, but first, you have to be able to imagine it—and the Remembering Process helps you do this with abilities you already have within you.

To get started, you need to understand—at least in a basic sense—two models of time: the Newtonian model and the Einsteinium model.

Sir Isaac Newton wrote that:

> Absolute, true, and mathematical time, in and of itself and of its own nature, without reference to anything external, flows uniformly and by another name is called duration. Relative, apparent, and common time is any sensible and external measure (precise or imprecise) of duration by means of motion; such a measure—for example, an hour, a day, a month, a year—is commonly used instead of true time.

In other words, time flows the same way for all observers and can be measured.

This is called Absolute Time, or "realist time." It's completely separate from the concept of space. It's as if there's one giant clock somewhere in the background of the universe that just keeps ticking away, regardless of what any of us are up to or what planet we're on.

Albert Einstein, however, thought there was another way of looking at time. He thought time and space were interconnected (he called it "space-time"), and that objects such as planets and stars warp the fabric of space-time. The bigger the object, the more it could warp—so planet Earth, for instance, would cause a big dip in the space-time continuum, like a big bowling ball in the middle of a trampoline. He called this theory General Relativity, and it was scientifically proven by NASA in 2007.

He named an additional theory, Special Relativity, to address that the speed of light is constant for all observers and nothing can move faster than the speed of light.

So time actually does move differently depending on where you are and what you're doing. The example most often used to illustrate this is called the "twin paradox"—if one twin is sent into space and travels at nearly the speed of light, when he comes back to Earth, he'll discover that his twin has aged much more than he has. Time affected them differently; the closer you are to the speed of light, the slower time moves. It's not something you'd be aware of—it wouldn't feel any slower because everything would be proportionally slowed, including your thoughts.

So what does this have to do with the Remembering Process?

It means that we can play with time. We don't have to accept that time passes just the same for us as it does for anyone else, nor that time is a fixed number constantly moving forward at a regular pace. We can be aware of the fact that time is relative to the observer—that maybe the past, present, and future aren't quite so fixed and separate from one another. So the Remembering Process could also be called "Einsteinium" remembering.

If you decide to study it, or even just give it some more thought, you may find that it changes your whole perspective, as it did for Gay Hendricks, Ph.D., a well-known psychologist and author of books about relationships and the body-mind connection (and the author of the Foreword of this book):

> My understanding of time was based on an outmoded, Newtonian paradigm. In a flash of insight I saw that Einstein's paradigm was the way time actually worked. I felt a shift of consciousness inside me, as if my very cells were re-arranging themselves around the new understanding. Everything changed in that moment, and from that day forward I've gotten everything done in half the time and had a great time doing it.
>
> As a result, I haven't been in a hurry in twenty years, although from the outside my life would appear to be wildly busier than it was when I had my big insight.

Einsteinium Remembering

Michelangelo felt he "freed" the *David* from the stone. The great artist said, "Every block of stone has a statue inside it, and it is the task of the sculptor to discover it." He also said, "I saw the angel in the marble and carved until I set him free."

Somewhere in the time and space continuum, the sculpture was complete and finished. He remembered the form, and allowed it to enter its new life.

I've had the honor, pleasure, and opportunity to create with a man like my co-author, Joe, who understands and practices the Remembering Process daily. I've seen him achieve amazing, tangible results as a writer, musician, speaker, friend, and all-around creator. Similar to Michelangelo's thoughts, Joe *starts* with the energy, the feeling, the threads, and then pulls the right elements toward him. He trusts what his soul and subconscious are telling him via these thin, gossamer threads.

This is truly Einsteinium.

Like Einstein found that a minute amount of mass could yield a massive amount of energy, we have found that small "particles" of belief, understanding, and feeling can explode into buildings, albums, books, relationships, and whole life paths. Few people I know grasp this. Most are waiting for large, overt signs in order to follow through with their dreams. These small particles of thought energy can mushroom into all and more of what our hearts seek.

The life you feel you could be living *lives now* somewhere in the time and space continuum, too. You feel that you could be living it because on some plane, you are! This process allows you to gently and smoothly remember those ideal traits and actions into your present perception of reality.

After I started practicing the Remembering Process, I wanted to see if there was any scientific evidence for what I was learning.

It should be no surprise that I was attracted to a book titled *Change Your Future Through Time Openings,* by Lucille and Jean-Pierre Garnier-Malet. It's a mind-stretching book about "time openings" that connect past, present, and future. In short, you can retrieve information from other times and use it to guide your present moment.

The authors talk about "doubles" in time. That means there is a "future you" as well as a "present you." The future you—your double—can send information back to you. This, of course, is what the Remembering Process is all about.

I don't think you need to read the book or understand physics to see that science is pointing in the direction that past, present, and future exist simultaneously. Knowing this might make it easier for you to make the leap into practicing the Remembering Process—and if so, wonderful. But I don't feel you need to know *anything* more to enjoy it right now.

Why not remember something you want right now?

— Joe

Einstein said it simply: "The distinction between past, present, and future is only an illusion, even if a stubborn one."

Along with this distinction, Einstein brought us the concept of relativity. To give a simple and personal illustration, one day my dog, Tupelo, got a desire to wander through a hole in my fence and check out some of my neighbors' yards. She was missing for only a few minutes, but it *felt* like hours.

That is relativity—time being expanded exponential-ly, or constricted, depending on perception. This is a tiny glimpse at how relative time is.

Our friend Mathes Jones (www.mathesjones.com) was going through a stressful time personally and professional-ly when she decided to make a big change in the way she dealt with the concept of time. This is how she explains it.

It doesn't take time . . . it takes mind.

This is what I discovered the year I decided to play around with time and prove to myself that, indeed, time was an illusion and not really the de-ciding factor.

Just prior to this decision, I had been reading books by Ernest Holmes, Dr. Joseph Murphy, and other New Thought authors because, in all honesty, I was struggling in just about every way.

And I was frustrated—not just with my life, but with how wonderful these authors made it all sound if I could just change my beliefs. Yet I knew intuitively this was the truth. I just had no idea how to do it.

At the time I was in sales, driving all over South-ern California every day. I covered hundreds of miles daily, and if you know anything about traffic there . . . well, you get the picture. Sometimes it took me three hours just to drive from my office in Beverly Hills to my home. That was my work life—all the while being a single mom with three children at home.

I simply *had* to prove that this stuff worked, so I did the most obvious thing I knew to do: I took my watch off.

I wrote out on a 3 by 5 index card: *I am always on time. I am always in the right place at the right time.* (Of course, this also meant *I am never late.*)

For the next year, I ran around from one end of SoCal to the next, appointment to appointment, without a watch to constantly check—L.A. to San Diego, up to the Valley, down to Orange County—often all in one day.

Some days I'd get into major traffic snarls and start to panic, afraid of what would happen—until I would remember, *I am always on time. I am always in the right place at the right time. I am never late.* Those words would immediately soothe and calm me, and I would relax again. And about as quickly as it appeared, the traffic would melt away and begin to flow.

In *every* case I was on time—with an occasional "twist."

Sometimes I would arrive at my appointment at what might be deemed "late," yet always, *always,* the receptionist would apologize because the person I was seeing was still in a meeting, hadn't come back from lunch, or was tied up for another five to ten minutes; it was always something.

"Do you mind waiting?" she'd ask.

I'd just smile and tell her no, not at all, and inside I would say to myself, *See? I'm never late.* Then whomever I had the appointment with would show up and apologize to me, too. (The Universe has such a sense of humor . . . if we will just play with it!)

Not that there weren't plenty of hair-raising moments when I would scare myself silly with my old story, yanking myself out of bliss and flow like the White Rabbit in *Alice in Wonderland* with my personal rendition of "Hurry, hurry! I'm late, I'm late, for a very important date!"

Eventually, though, that tune gave way to a new song and a new way of being with myself in this thing we call time. And rather than using time to punish myself, or push and pull, I transformed it to work harmoniously for me. Or, as Gay Hendricks suggests in *The Big Leap*, I discovered that *I'm where time comes from.*

Reproduced by permission of Mathes Jones.

In his book *The Big Leap*, Gay Hendricks writes at length about Einstein's concept of relativity and how it affects our perception of time. When you're running on Einstein Time, he explains, your experience of time changes, and you can even gain the ability to generate more time by changing the way you occupy space. Einstein used a simple example to demonstrate the relativity of time: an hour with your beloved feels like a minute, whereas a minute on a hot stove feels like an hour, and that has a powerful impact on the way we live.

As Gay writes in *The Big Leap*:

If you are forced to sit on a hot stove, you become preoccupied with trying *not* to occupy the space you're in. You withdraw your consciousness toward your core, contracting away from the pain of contact with the stove. The act of contracting your awareness away from space makes time congeal. It seems to slow down and harden into a solid mass. The more you cringe from the pain, the slower time gets.

When you're embracing your beloved, though, your awareness flows in the opposite direction. When you're with your beloved, your every cell yearns to be one with him or her. Your awareness flows out toward your periphery. You want to occupy every possible smidgen of space in the yearned-for present. When you're in love, you relax into the space around you and in you, and as your consciousness expands into space, time disappears.

That's why we don't look at our watches when we're having a great time. We don't care about the time. On the other hand, when we're feeling miserable and sitting in the doctor's waiting room, we stare at the clock—at the second hand, even, which seems to be moving at a snail's pace just to taunt us! This is not the space we want to occupy. We want to be feeling good again, back in that moment with our beloved where nothing else mattered. Gay writes: "When you're willing to occupy all space, time simply disappears. You're everywhere all at once, there's no place to get to, and everywhere you are it's exactly the right time."

When you are creating from "Einsteinium remembering," you mentally occupy a space where your being energetically expands. In your mind, you enter the place where the music (literally and figuratively) is sourced from—some people will say that's communicating with God or connecting with the Divine. It's a place of love and inspiration, and it helps you to enter the unified field of consciousness.

"The *what?*" you may ask.

The unified field is a state where you feel connected to the entire universe—where you no longer feel separate from other people, but you feel that all people are part of one another and can share a global consciousness. You feel connected to the earth, the air you breathe, the animals and plants and "things," as well as the intangibles, such as spirituality and time. You no longer experience time as just a linear thing chugging ever forward, but you know there are pieces of yourself in history as well as in the future, all over the world. You stop worrying about not having enough time, because you know that time is malleable, and you don't have to accept the stopwatch mentality driving most of the world. You trust that you are already in the right place at the right time and that you will continue to grow toward the life you are meant to have.

We enter this unified state by resolving the paradox in our mind and heart. Our desires, even when from a state of duality and want, are homing signals back to the unified field. They are an alarm system that says we've lost our home and our peaceful state. If we feel we lack something, then surely we're being called to remember the place from which nothing is lacking, and nothing is everything. From this place, we can breathe into existence that which we put our energy toward.

There is no wanting here, for the kingdom of heaven is already in our hands and hearts. You could call it the *Tao*, the Chinese principle that guides the way of life. If you start with the premise that there's an aspect of divinity in all of us, then we're connected to everything and everyone, and there's no need to want because everything is already within our reach.

The Tao of Remembering

Sometimes we get thwarted from our efforts to evolve into our higher states because it's hard for our animal bodies to maintain this energy state. Adopting a new, eternal mind-set tends to be a gradual possibility. The unified state does not come all at once, but as Lao-tzu suggests in the Tao Te Ching, "less and less do you need to force things."

This means that the door is open for those of us who are late bloomers and slower learners—good news, indeed.

Understanding the relevance of the unified state will strengthen your ability to utilize the Remembering Process and allow you to work *with* the Law of Attraction—not against it—although, as I will discuss later, there are benefits to the process regardless.

Time is a funny thing.

Whenever Daniel and I needed to make a decision about the music we were working on, we stopped and went to the future. When I was invited to be on the cover of *Austin All Natural* magazine in early 2011, I wasn't sure what the cover should look like. The editor had left it up to me and said that he wanted me to be on the cover in three months.

At that point, we weren't planning to create an album so quickly. The original goal when I hired Daniel to help me was to make an album by the end of the year. But now that the cover-issue opportunity was in play, we were trying to remember what we did.

Could I make my first album in only three months?

Remembering made this easier. There was a built-in assumption that the cover was done. It had to be if we were remembering it. All we were doing now is fine-tuning our vision. What did that cover look like?

As Daniel and I explored the possibilities, we "remembered" the cover. In other words, we pretended the cover had already been printed and the magazine distributed. We looked into our future mind and tried to see what the cover looked like. We just played with the idea, not attached to the outcome or to being right. We were allowing ourselves to free-associate.

"I see a hazy photo of me with the harp guitar," I said. "But I'm not sure. Maybe it was me with a new car, or a different guitar."

As a result of this remembering, I created a five-track album in three months, titled *Blue Healer*. And I ended up on the cover with me holding the 1915 Gibson harp guitar pretty much as we remembered it.

This is astonishing. To go from zero to new album in three months, especially for a newbie like me, was miraculous.

How'd we do it?

We remembered it.

— Joe

Just as Newton didn't invent gravity but gave it a new name, we didn't invent this paradigm in any way, shape, or form. The Remembering Process is a new mental model that can help us ease into this timeless paradigm—the unified state—from which all blessings and peace flow. It's a way of using your mind and heart's desires as a portal to connect with the great, mysterious, connected universe.

By-products of this path include a desire to share, along with feelings of well-being, abundance, possibility, and a wonderful, prosperous existence.

Creating Remembering Letters

When I thought about my own goals, I wrote a Re-membering Letter:

> *I remember that when I took that next step of prosperity, peace, and calm, I either cut my hair shorter or started wearing it a bit differently. I remember using a new product in my hair, maybe American Crew po-made. It had a very masculine smell. I remember the feeling of pride that I was calm and clear. I remember that my shirts were done at the cleaners. I remember tearing off the little ID tags, and the stiff and clean feeling of wearing a fresh shirt. I remember . . .*

On the surface, that paragraph may not seem to have anything to do with furthering my stated goals of improved prosperity, peace, and calm—but those little details are an accessible jumping-off point when you don't "remember" the bigger picture yet. I might not have been sure exactly how I would reach my goals, but I could "remember" the sensory details that I would associate with success and a peaceful feeling.

I suggest that you play with writing Remembering Letters, too.

You may want to dedicate a specific notebook or journal to this purpose, but don't let it hold you back if you don't have one handy. You can write these letters to your-self in any manner you wish: on scraps of paper, on the computer, in the margins of your date book . . . wherever feels natural for you. It's important to just dig in and do it rather than trying to do it "perfectly." Your letters are your letters, and they don't need to be written beautifully or po-etically. They don't even need to be spelled correctly. The idea is for you to commit to words the sensory details that will help you "remember" attaining your goals.

Many times throughout the process of writing this book, I remembered the results: I remembered getting an e-mail from my editor saying, "Congratulations! You've done it." I remembered seeing the book on bookstore shelves and people leafing through copies. I didn't have to remember exactly how I got there yet, but I remembered the book as being whole and finished and stunning. That gave me more confidence every time I sat down to write, because I knew that in the end, it was going to be just as I'd remembered it. I didn't have to worry that I might not finish it, or that it might not be good enough. Joe and I both knew that it was going to be wonderful and help people—we knew because we remembered it—so it took away much of the anxiety inherent in the process and al-lowed us to write freely. We didn't even have to get it right the first time; we knew that it might take rounds of editing to get our message just the way we intended it, but in the end, it was going to be right.

Here are some questions you might want to think about when you start your Remembering Letters. On the day you achieved your desired outcome:

- What season was it?
- What time of day?

- What did you eat that day?

- What were you wearing?

- What objects were around you?

- How did you feel?

- Was anyone with you?

- Who congratulated you?

- What sounds did you hear?

- What scents were in the air?

- Where did you go?

- Was it similar to any other feelings?

- What part was even better than you had imagined?

One of the cool things about building memories like this is that they tend to build their own stories—one piece of a story will lead you to the next, and the next. If at first it feels phony, that's okay. Trust it anyway, and write it down. It probably *will* feel phony in the beginning, but less so as you get the hang of this type of remembering.

You get to write your own destiny. Like the writer/director of a movie, you get to decide how things will look, who the cast of characters will be, what they will say, and how they will change. If you decide later that you don't like one aspect or another, you get to go to the editing room and change it . . . just like a director can reshoot the ending of a movie, you can rewrite your Remembering Letters, or write a series of new ones that better home in on just how you envision your life.

My Remembering Letters for this book were actually a series of e-mails between Joe and me—I was lucky to have a terrific partner to "play" with in this regard. If you have someone in your life who is supportive and on the same wavelength, then you may want to share your letters with him or her, too, and build off each other. If not, then keep them for yourself and watch how your perceptions may change over time. Be an interested observer, like a researcher studying the effects of the Remembering Process. After writing these letters to yourself for a few weeks, do you feel any differences? Do you notice yourself becoming more confident in your ability to attain your desired outcomes? More creative? More at peace?

If writing doesn't feel natural to you, you might try recording your "letters" instead. Talk into any recording device—your phone or MP3 player may even have one built in. Talk about the same sorts of details you'd write. In either case, saying it out loud or writing it down, you're committing the thoughts to memory and encouraging your imagination to come out and play some more.

It's akin to keeping a dream journal. If you've never tried this, give it a shot and see how it can also change your perception: You may not remember many of your dreams, but if you keep a notebook and a flashlight next to your bed for a few weeks and write down everything you do remember, you'll likely find that it changes your whole thought process about dreaming. Whereas before, you might have remembered just one or two dreams a week, now you may easily remember one or more dreams every morning, just because you've trained your brain to retain the information you didn't even know you could access before. You unlocked a whole untapped area of your mind just by acknowledging it, expecting it, and writing down whatever it told you.

There is power in writing things down and saying things out loud. Give it a try with the Remembering Process and see where it takes you.

Now that you have a basic understanding of the Remembering Process, we can delve deeper into the thought processes behind it and how it relates to the Law of Attraction.

THE LAW OF ATTRACTION AND THE TROUBLE WITH WANTING

"Logic will get you from A to B.
Imagination will take you everywhere."

— Albert Einstein

The act of "wanting" separates us from that which we think we want. When we "want" an outcome, we create an immediate barrier to it. When we think we "need" the outcome, that barrier becomes even greater. The perceived need triggers a fear of not having and the fear creates a fight-or-flight response in our bodies. Let's take the example of an important job interview. We become anxious—*I need to get this job!*—and our brain interprets that need as if it really were needed, just like air, water, and food. The brain thinks, *I need to get this job, or I will not survive.* At that point, we're really focused only on basic survival.

The fight-or-flight response is a hardwired reaction to stress geared to protect us from harm, dating back to when stress meant that a tiger was chasing you or about to swipe your baby from your hut. Your sympathetic nervous system and adrenal-cortical system go into overdrive, releasing massive doses of adrenaline, noradrenaline, and other chemicals intended to help you either run away really fast or find the superhuman strength needed to fight off a deadly predator.

It's very hard to thrive when your body is releasing the same chemicals it would release if you were fighting a saber-toothed tiger. Now you're in the job interview sweating, hyperventilating, and unable to focus on small tasks because your brain is on hyper-alert, waiting for that tiger to roar so you can figure out where it is.

But you can turn this around by taking a different approach. As poet Rainer Maria Rilke said, "Wishes are recollections coming from the future." As you "remember" that your desired outcome actually does exist somewhere in the time and space continuum, there is no need for tension, fear, or doubt of any kind. Somewhere, that job already belongs to you. You can gently and gracefully call that reality into your consciousness because it's already ongoing. This ease allows these experiences to arrive into your "field" without stress. Your field encompasses everything you are: your physical, mental, and spiritual self. The only effort is in working toward living in a state of unified consciousness.

In other words, we willfully create our inner ecology such that a unified state of being may flourish and grow.

Eva Pierrakos, a renowned psychic channeler from Vienna, gave a series of 258 lectures from 1957 until her death in 1979. These lectures were delivered in a trance state, and she attributed them to a spirit known only as The Guide. Collectively, they became known as the Pathwork lectures and are available in their entirety for free at www.pathwork.org. Lecture #112, "Humanity's Relationship to Time," illuminates how humans unwittingly set up their own barriers:

> Fear of death causes a backward movement opposed to the natural movement of time which is steady, harmonious flow. If you can feel into its rhythm, you will be in harmony. You can do so by being in time in the only meaningful way, using each moment and incident for growth. Not straining away from the future, you will not have to fear it. Not pulling away from the present, you will utilize it well, so that it will not seem desirable to strain away from it. This is being, even if it is not yet the highest state of being. It is the state of being commensurate with the dimension of time you live in.
>
> Once in this state, you follow the natural flow. The wave of time will bring you naturally and gracefully into the next extended dimension, which you fear so much because you cannot yet prove its reality. Your very haste, on the one hand, to get into the new dimension, and your fear of the unknown, on the other, are reactions to what seems so uncertain to a part of your personality. With these reactions you restrain the natural movement and create tension, setting your soul forces to work in opposing directions. The result is stagnation of growth, as well as lack of the full experience of each "now."

Foundation. Reprinted by permission of the Pathwork Foundation. www.pathwork.org)

Consequently, if we are to work in harmony with the Law of Attraction, we want to learn to work from this unified state as much as possible—eliminating the pull of wanting, which snaps us out of it.

The sensation you're looking for is a peaceful one, an absence of pulling. It's an absence of doing, an absence of wanting. Why would you pine for a turkey sandwich when you have two hands around one, mid-bite? That's the sensation.

Making small changes in your language changes everything. Joe calls statements that start with "I want," "I intend," and similar phrases *victim statements.* They imply that you do not have, and therefore are not whole. They are statements that suggest that you'll have to fight for the things you don't have because you are coming to it from a place of neediness. Saying "I remember" changes the entire landscape because now you're no longer a victim; you have everything you want. Maybe it's not yet in your possession at this moment, but it's yours. It's coming soon. You don't have to fight; it's much easier than wanting.

Ever since I appeared in the movie *The Secret*, people all over the world ask me about attracting everything from relationships to money. I even created a Miracles Coaching program to help individuals understand and use the principles I teach.

The Remembering Process is a way to speed up the Law of Attraction. You are already attracting. What you have is what you attracted. Congratulations. You are powerful.

But what if you don't like what you attracted? What if you want to attract something else?

You can use the Remembering Process to not only focus on what you want next, but to also actually pull it to you. By "remembering" that you attracted your goal, you more deeply convince yourself that it's not just possible, but that it *already* happened. This increased energy fuels the Law of Attraction to kick into gear at a higher level.

For example, let's say that you want to attract better health. In the traditional way of attracting, you might recite affirmations or sit and meditate on your chosen goal. That's all well and good. But imagine adding remembering to the mix.

Now you leap past the actual experience of having better health. Now you know you somehow obtained it or attracted it. It has to exist because you're remembering it.

What you can do from this playful place of remembering is ask yourself questions, such as, *How did I create this healthy version of me?* It doesn't matter if your answers are fuzzy. After all, you are remembering. Your answers might open you to a new possibility.

Here's the kicker: By remembering that what you want (a healthier you) did, in fact, come to be, you're adding energy to the very thing you want to attract.

You are speeding up the process.

You are creating—or remembering—miracles.

— Joe

The way to the unified space is to be totally thrilled in this moment as if it were here. Or as Andy Warhol is quoted saying in a picture posted on my studio wall: "You have to be willing to get happy about nothing."

To agree with the moment right now, knowing that all that we seek is within a network of energy that we are very much part of, brings that desire to the present. The final leap is to know that it actually *is* right here, right now.

Many self-help methods and disciplines have alluded to this problem of wanting. *Psycho-Cybernetics,* for example, written by Maxwell Maltz in 1960, referred to the "intention tremor" of trying too hard to thread a small needle. This is a great metaphor for what happens when we live in the duality of wanting and fear of lacking. Our efforts to "thread the needle" of our desires creates an unnatural tension and awkward, misguided aim to our efforts.

Remembering that we already have that which we think we want allows a certain kind of breathing, an easing of physical and mental tension, and an allowing of the more mysterious universal energies to flow to and from what we put our attention on. Instead of doing and wanting, we simply apply a certain kind of attention to an outcome. The "texture" of this feels more like a fond memory than anything else.

I remember the elements first. I remember that this section of the book was fun and fluid. I remember that it outlined the purpose and positive reasons to get clear about what you desire, even if letting go of that desire is the next step to having it. What a paradox! I remember that the book had lots of quotes and that it came together easily. I remember that I went to sleep very early this week so I was fresh when

I woke up at 5 A.M. I remember that I was terrifically productive.

The Remembering Process, like the Law of Attraction, is essentially a vibration game. You know when you've met someone who seems happy and confident and welcoming, you might say that the person has a "good vibe"? Well, that's the key to a better, more successful life: giving and receiving the right "vibes," or vibrations. Another word for this is *radiance*—some people just radiate positive energy.

We've come to this Earth to play with these vibrations and figure out how to put our proverbial hands on the steering wheel and throttle of life—the vibration wave machine, so to speak. We vibrate and resonate with thoughts, ideas, and actions; and they either harmonize or clash. It's like playing music. We want to be in tune with a certain style, a certain frequency, certain chords and rhythms. So we learn it. We learn the *vibe.* For instance, we can say that a song has a "country vibe." Many people are born in and of a country vibe, yet some of my favorite country musicians were born in the city. I have a sort of Southern vibe, even though I was born a Jewish kid in New York. I still feel love and respect for those roots.

But I love Texas—it's home. The weather suits my clothes, as the old folk song says. I'm just at home here. I like the weather; I like the food. I like the music and my boots. I finally found "home" when I moved to Texas. I love to visit my family up north in New York, but there's something about being here in the South. It's a frequency and vibration that calls to me. My soul mixes with it.

In many cases, people come into the world already tapped into a certain kind of energy. Have you ever met someone like Michael Jordan who is an athlete not only in his body and actions, but down in his soul? How else could someone once considered too short to play basketball back in his high-school days eventually go on to become an icon of the game? It's like his whole energy field is athletic.

Similarly, some people give off wealth energy. There are plenty of wealthy people who, although born poor, learn rich vibes and manifest wealth.

And it's not a just a shrewdness of mind. Put these individuals anywhere in the world and something in them will attract plenty. Or middle-class vibes—those energies are there, too. You can see it in people.

Which vibes do you really want to learn?

I remember that I bought my Ferrari from Tad Cole, a broker Joe knows. I remember the calipers were red and that the F430 was the way to go. I remember that the car was a token of love to myself, a direct result of creating enough positivity inward that it spilled over to those around me. I remember that buying a Rolex was the first anchor in this chain. However, it's not about "things" as much as it's about treating oneself like a king or queen. This assertion of self-worth makes it easier and easier to act regally toward others.

One of the first things I did was create a folder of my accomplishments and great notes I've received from others over the years. Celebrating myself was a stretch. I had somehow lost the ability to cheer for myself, so it helped to read about others celebrating me. It reminded me that I was good at what I do and have many abilities. This habit allowed me to relax enough to start to play with creativity and radical possibility in a way I'd never known existed.

I remember that reading my own book continued to help me. I remember that it helped many people. Expressing these ideas the best I could, even imperfectly, was a gift I gave myself and those searching for this key to their own progression.

You can manifest lots of love or sex or friends in your life. All of these vibrations are available. People who create any of these things for themselves have learned to repeat and broadcast those particular vibrations. With each of these desires, there are ways that you "hang"—ways that you just "be" that create a particular lifestyle.

A breakthrough thought is that you don't have to be born with it. You can be a musician, a mathematician, a magician. You don't necessarily have to live what you seem to have been raised into or for. People prove this all of the time.

Life can be a game of deciding which things you were given that you want to really relax into, and which ones you want to find the dial for and tune in to a change.

The Remembering Process is a way to tap into those vibrations. It's a quantum—not linear—approach to drawing yourself into that universal energy, and the most powerful tool I've found for tapping into that power to draw in your desires. *Quantum* in this case means that you've leaped in understanding from the commonplace reality to one of enormous and expansive possibilities. It's the difference between what you see as reality with your eyes and what is possible with your human imagination.

The different energies are out there, and you can find their channel, like a radio station you tune in to. The Remembering Process opens your spiritual radio receiver to receive from whatever station you are tuning in to; and you bolster that decision with the TV you watch, the friends you keep, the conversations you indulge in—for good or bad.

For example, if you're like me and want to play country music, you could tune in to and receive a strong country vibe. Go to lots of shows. Talk to lots of people who love country music. Listen to the great albums. Wear a hat, perhaps. (I look funny in a cowboy hat, but you know what I mean.) It's a way to put yourself in that vibration. Keep in mind that you don't have to live in Texas for 30 years to really be at home. You only have to tap into your "Southernism," which is in your vibes.

I have a friend who has British vibes, even though she's from Kansas. She really lives it. It's the frequency she's happiest in; it's her comfort zone. She even uses various English words and mannerisms. She would rather say *pram* than *baby carriage,* for example. It's a strong assertion of self-creation.

Find the radio station that you most want to receive. You just have to be able to stay with it. Then keep choosing it.

In time, people around you get used to certain stations emanating from you. If you've been tuning your "receiver" into WPOOR radio, you become known for that vibration, and forces seen and unseen. It's okay to want to make money. It's okay to want "stuff." As Pat O'Bryan of Practical Metaphysics writes, "There's nothing inherently wrong with 'stuff.' Material objects are neutral. It's the lust for stuff that will make you miserable."

There's desperation in that lust—a sense of lack that marketers play into very well. They want you to believe that you can't be happy until you have that car, that beauty cream, that pair of shoes. Instead, you can take back the power *and* still have your stuff. You can be happy right now, regardless of whether it's in your current possession or not.

And you can invite it into your possession by simply re-membering that it's yours. Don't waste any energy worry-ing about whether you deserve it, have earned it, or if it's too silly or materialistic or whatever. If something vibrates with you, it's yours. You have an abundant life and the abil-ity to attract whatever you want into it.

As you change your mind-set, you must keep asserting where it is you want to "live." Some of us are orphans in that spiritual or creative sense. We are not raised with the language, understanding, or support to do what it is we want to do.

In his book *It's Never Crowded Along the Extra Mile,* Dr. Wayne Dyer recounts growing up on his own in foster care. This experience forced him to develop confidence and an ability to create his own reality, which became his modus operandi for his entire career. Dr. Dyer is famous for saying, "You'll see it when you believe it."

The Remembering Process helps you believe in your goals or desires in a way that nothing else I've found can. When you remember that it's already done, some part of you just accepts that you are fully capable. The fear mecha-nism releases, and your best work can unfold.

Self-development is a gift, not a burden. The need to do it by your own bootstraps is important at different stages of development. Children get to a point where they want to pour the milk themselves, and this translates to an adult's spiritual growth. Your growth will eventually take you to a place that surpasses where your parents, friends, or anyone else can take you.

That's when you have to tap into your deeper wisdom. You attune your receiver to the reality you feel and the de-sire deep in your heart, and let those frequencies give you a series of clues to unfold that reality into being. At a certain point, a critical mass in vibration occurs, and people will begin to associate you fully with your newly chosen reality.

A few years ago, I was struggling and using identity phrases like "poor musician" and "starving artist," but now I tell the musicians I mentor to run at the sound of those types of clichés. There is a profound lack of creativity and work ethic at the heart of those stereotypes. There are so many successful, industrious musicians and artists. I've been able to successfully *remember* my life as a productive, high-earning album producer. The shift in memory was fuzzy at first, slowly got clearer, and then it became crystal clear.

Not long ago, I was honored to be a judge during a business-plan demo at the Acton School of Business's MBA program. I leaned over and whispered to one of my fellow judges, who manages a billion-dollar venture-capital fund, that my past reality was laughing in awe of where I had arrived. For me, that event signified the full fruition of my status as a spiritual receiver of industry and wealth.

Being in Gratitude

One way to ease yourself into a vibration you're not currently in is through gratitude. If you feel alone and are at rock bottom with any of your negative patterns, gratitude may seem far out of reach.

Reach for it anyway. Find something, however small, to feel grateful about, and work at building on it. Take inventory of your life and write down the things about it that are good: Do you have good health, friends, food to eat, a beloved pet, a hobby you enjoy, a cherished belonging, a working car, a great coffeemaker, a good last dental checkup, a special talent, an aunt who called you on your birthday, two arms, a warm blanket, clean drinking water, a nice library? Look for things to feel grateful about every day, all around you, from the sights you see in nature to the guy at the bakery who threw in an extra cookie in your order.

Being in gratitude makes everything work better, including the Remembering Process. No matter the circumstances, you can find gratitude in the thought that this is how badly you wanted to assert your spiritual power in the direction of healing and change. In other words, you are so committed to creating change and healing that you need a low place to start to really map out the path for you and your fellow seekers, so you can be thankful for that low place. Are there other explanations to why you may be in a tight spot of fear or pain? Perhaps you're sick, heartbroken, or need to learn a particular lesson—so notice which story or explanation inspires you most to action.

Sometimes we need to break things down and look for proof. It's good to go to a doctor for tests when you suspect something is wrong with your health, for instance. And it's good to research someone's history before going into business with him or her. Other times, it behooves us to live the story that raises our vibration the highest, without any proof that it's real or that it will "work."

If you are gifted with faith in yourself, your path, or a higher power, you know what I mean. So if it helps you to believe that the reason you're at this low point is because you needed a fresh start to build a new kind of life, then go with that thought.

All the time that you could spend debating the truth or relative untruth of an idea, you could be basking in the glow of its inspiration.

The Upper-Limit Problem

> "Man's mind, once stretched by a new idea,
> never regains its original dimensions."
>
> — Oliver Wendell Holmes

In opening ourselves up to our desires, besides not letting ourselves know what we want, we may run into what is known as the "upper-limit problem," where we create our own glass ceilings. What is the Upper-Limit Problem (ULP)? Gay Hendricks describes it as the following:

> The ULP is the human tendency to put the brakes on our positive energy when we've exceeded our unconscious thermostat setting for how good we can feel, how successful we can be, and how much love we can feel. The essential move we all need to master is learning to handle more positive energy, success, and love.

I have, at every juncture of positive change in my life, had to raise the bar on what I would tolerate in terms of happiness. "Tolerate happiness?" you ask. Yes. My capacity to allow for great feelings has needed expansion. Like a thermostat, it's been set to what I thought was a "normal" state of fulfillment. Sometimes it's been set to some really nice-feeling states. Still, each time I've been called forth into my deeper creative fulfillment, I've had to open up to feeling better. I have some taboos about being too happy. You probably do, too. And when we don't realize this, we start to unconsciously sabotage great things as they happen. Each time you reach a new height of fulfillment, you are likely to be met with a challenge to clear out old beliefs. This will allow you to make a hospitable soil for your new-found happiness to grow in.

The Remembering Process helps you break through imaginary barriers to success. Whether you view this from a cosmic or neural orientation doesn't matter. I'm biased to the cosmic, but both work. The bottom line is that the Remembering Process can unlock some of our human potential. As constructs in the brain, barriers can be eliminated.

Even the concept of time is a construct. "We believe that time emerged during the Big Bang, and if time can emerge, it can also disappear—that's just the reverse effect," says Professor Gary Gibbons, a cosmologist at Cambridge University.

And new discoveries of subatomic particles by leading scientists continue to evolve our understanding of the cosmos. For example, Jeff Forshaw, a professor at Manchester University, suggests that a most recent discovery, if confirmed, would make it possible in theory to "send information into the past."

But why wait?

I remember that my "stories" about time and whether or not I had enough of it melted, and I felt plenty of time to do what I needed to do in life.

There's so much we don't know about time, and our notion of it is very two-dimensional for the most part. Playing with time far past our goals as we do in the Remembering Process seems effective. And we *are* playing here.

A Sense of Play, Lightness, and Openness

Remember that anything you want already exists in various states of development. Effort or worrying pushes it away. Enjoying each aspect of it as equally existent, savoring and observing the qualities of that phase, allows you to stay open and just "be" with the energy that *is* that thing *now*. It's like enjoying a child's whole development and soaking it in, instead of pushing or pulling for the child to be an adult.

It unlocks your ability to enjoy the finished version *now* in time and space. If you can be with the current energy states of your vision in an observant and open manner, then the energy of that vision, of that thing you want, is able to dance, move, skip, and grow.

The Remembering Process is similar to playing jazz music—the more you practice and open up, the more you take care of the details. Also, the more you remain playful, the more you can experience the spirit of the technique.

Play begins by making room for the practice. For example, I worked on this book Mondays, Wednesdays, and Fridays between noon and one o'clock. I set the time aside as a discipline, but I also focus on making that time sweet for myself, making room for play in the process of writing. Our pleasure and pain centers direct our perception of time—remember that "time flies when you're having fun."

One way we can move into the unified state is to remind ourselves that we have the ability to create our experience of a given moment. We can create a spirit of play rather than stay in nonproductive states, such as worry. And "Worry is a misuse of the imagination," says Steve Chandler, author of the book *Fearless*.

Remembering offers lightness—the opposite of the heaviness of lack found in "I want, I want." Heaviness clogs the mechanism.

Shortly before getting a massage, I was telling my massage therapist about the writing of this book, and she asked, "What is the Remembering Process?"

"It's an advanced visualization technique," I replied. "You go past what you want to create, off into the future, and you try to remember the details of how you created what you want."

"That makes sense because the future already exists."

"Exactly! Knowing that what you want already exists gives you faith and power. Now you simply and playfully 'remember' how you did it."

I went on and told her I was developing a line of shoes. I don't know how to do it, but since it already exists in the future, I just see if I can recall the steps to get there from here.

"That means in the future your massage is already over," she pointed out, smiling.

"Yes . . . but I still want one now."

— Joe

Remembering involves feeling joyful now as though our goal or object of desire were in front of us and in our possession. We can work on creating a unified time field by soothing and enticing our brain to find the joy and play in the moments in front of us.

I remember that the book got progressively more fun and easy as I created more joy in the process.

In another example, if you were to observe when Joe and I get together to create music, you would see two guys hitting a state of pure potential and imagination. We dream big and think big—and "remember" big. It takes this sense of childlike wonder, faith, and curiosity. As Einstein once said, "The pursuit of truth and beauty is a sphere of activity in which we are permitted to remain children all of our lives."

The Remembering Process is a gentle hand leading us to the sandbox and playground of reality. The most enlightened I can imagine is to lovingly dance in the unknown, toward a soulful expression of the truth in each moment, to move gently but with full spirit toward our destiny.

This is the best use of this earthly tour of duty. Enlightenment is in flux at all times. There is no end and no beginning. That's why we can play in the infinite *now* where there is nothing to attain because we have already attained it. And we can let go of it and everything in between.

If the Divine is in all of us, then enlightenment is inherently attained. The Remembering Process can certainly help us live a life that is informed by the Divine within us. There is no single human with a leg up on this enlightenment. You have the same "right" to that enlightenment as the greatest thinkers you can name. You just have to perceive the divinity within and actively seek to live its wisdom.

Of course, it will still work if you are closed and curmudgeonly.

Like a chess game, you don't need metaphysical faith to reverse engineer it. Chess legend Garry Kasparov described how he would be many steps ahead of his current situation. "Normally, I would calculate three to five moves," he said. "You don't need more . . . but I can go much deeper if it is required."

Remembering can help you reimagine what would need to happen to achieve the desired outcome. And to get to that jazz-inspired state of creating your life, you will definitely need a sense of play. Observing children playing can help you adapt the energy you'll need to open up to the Remembering Process. Notice their level of trust and how much they enjoy the energy of whatever they're engaged with, such as "truck" energy when they're playing with trucks. In other words, they agree to a world inside that opens up to them when they play with the truck.

Throughout my life I've been influenced by various authors. Whether Mark Twain, Ralph Waldo Emerson, or P.T. Barnum, they came alive for me through their books. I still cherish their words. Reading them is like awakening a friend from sleep, who speaks to me with great wisdom and compassion, love and light. How I wish I could have had dinner with any of them!

Today I collect signed works by those influential authors. I have a photograph of Mark Twain, hand signed by him. I also have signed books by P.T. Barnum and a collection of Emerson's writing.

I look at these reminders that these men actually walked the earth and a part of me transports in time, mentally, and sits with them. I don't know how to explain it. It's very real. *I remember sitting at a dinner table with Barnum and Tom Thumb and their wives. There was stimulating conversation, laughter, shared stories, food, and wine.* It's as real to me as writing these words is right now.

I've also been reading biographies of these individuals, and when I do, I "remember" knowing them. Obviously, I never met any of them. They all died decades before I was ever born. But I own evidence of their lives. And this evidence gives me a touchstone to mentally "remember" talking to them, learning from them, and so much more.

That's one aspect of the Remembering Process. I can remember what never happened in order to learn something new. Who knows, I may write a novel of all this remembering of being with Twain, Emerson, and Barnum. In that way, I can profit from what I learned as I remembered. I would open a door to a new dimension and discover what was there all along,

I use this same mental process to go into the future—months to years past this moment—and remember what I did to get to the future.

For example, my goal as I write this is to be on the cover of *Rolling Stone* magazine for my music CD *Strut!* To help me visualize this end result, I hired a graphic designer to put me on the cover and send me the image. I then printed it out and looked at it every day. It's a way to program my mind for success.

But here's what I do differently, thanks to the Remembering Process: I imagine the cover is already printed, distributed, and on the stands. In fact, it happened a few months ago; it's now old news. I think of the memory with fondness and pride.

I remember talking to people about it. I recall people on the street stopping to thank and congratulate me. I recall the sales that came from <u>Strut!</u> as a result, which made it a chart-topping hit on <u>Billboard.</u>

> I remember all this because it's real in some way in the future, in my mind, in another dimension, or in a parallel universe. It's real and I'm simply recalling it, as a way to call it into being.
>
> *I also shared my success at my next meeting with Twain, Emerson, and Barnum. They sat around, smoking cigars, smiling big, and laughing with me. I remember Twain asking me what a CD was and Emerson smiling knowingly as Barnum replied that it was a new kind of animal found in Africa that charmed children at night so they could sleep better.*
>
> I love remembering such sweetness!
>
> — Joe

Remembering big, zany, playful aspects also helps jog creativity and higher thinking. On our way to tapping into the cosmos, we're opening up our brain chemistry. Side effects include positive thinking and feeling happy and inspired.

We can remember that things do not have to be such a grind. We can remember joy and spontaneity. We can remember that these wonderful feelings belong to us and can be part of our everyday lives if we claim them.

If you're unhappy, use the Remembering Process to remember how you became happy again. If you're already happy, use it to remember being even happier. Aren't we lucky that happiness isn't finite?

With a deeper understanding of what the Remembering Process is about, let's move on to the fun part: how to put it into practice!

HOW TO DO THE REMEMBERING PROCESS

"Music and higher mathematics share some obvious kinship. The practice of both requires a lengthy apprenticeship, talent, and no small amount of grace. Both seem to spring from some mysterious workings of the mind. Logic and system are essential for both, and yet each can reach a height of creativity beyond the mechanical."

— Frederick Pratter

Being a musician makes it easy to compare the Remembering Process to learning to play jazz. Both arise from a spontaneous set of influences.

To play music, you need to be in the moment while also creating, hearing, feeling, and remembering the moments that are *about* to happen. You have to be in the heart of the note you are playing and, at the same time, already feeling what has not yet happened, but will. You learn technique and also when to let go of technique. The more you enter the "jazz and remembering zone," the more at home you become.

Also, there is a collective power in playing jazz, as well as in "remembering," with other like-minded people. You start feeding off one another and building on each other's memories. If you can find people who are open to trying this process with you, you may find that they can "help" you remember things you may have forgotten. You might say, "I remember that I took a vacation after I finished this project," and they can fill in the details for you: "Oh, yes! I remember you came back with a great tan," or "I remember you went on a Ferris wheel while you were away."

Joe was given an interesting opportunity to put this into practice when Jack Canfield (of Chicken Soup for the Soul fame) asked him to give a talk at a Transformational Leadership Council conference in Canada in 2012. We were in the process of writing this book, and Joe had showed the manuscript to Jack. Jack liked it so much that he asked Joe to give a talk about it . . . and Joe was nervous. First, the book wasn't even finished yet, and he hadn't ever spoken publicly about the Remembering Process before. This would be a presentation in front of some of the most well-known leaders in the personal-development field, and he was afraid of failing.

In the car on the way to the airport, he was complaining to his wife, Nerissa, about his nerves when it occurred to him that he had a technique to use that could help—the Remembering Process!

"Would you mind doing the Remembering Process with me right now?" he asked her.

"What do you mean? How would that work?" she asked.

"Well, we're no longer on our way to the airport . . . we're coming back."

For the rest of the ride, they talked about how well the conference had gone: how much he enjoyed it, and how he saw the audience's eyes grow bright and people sitting forward in their chairs as they "got it." It changed his whole energy, and he was able to get on that plane with confidence.

One of my dear friends, artist and coach Ann Rea (www .artistswhothrive.com), helps me with the Remembering Process consistently just by what she calls me: "Grammy Dan." It's been her nickname for me ever since she found out that one of my biggest goals in life is to win a Grammy Award. When Ann e-mails me, she always addresses it to "Grammy Dan," and I always remind her to have her red dress ready so she can accompany me to the ceremony. Supportive friends like Ann can not only help keep you on track with what's important to you, but can also elevate the process to something more joyful and hopeful.

And you can do the same for someone else. Next time a loved one confides in you about fears or insecurities, "remember" for him or her. It can be so reassuring to hear someone say, "I remember how well it went for you," rather than, "I hope it will go well," or even "I know you'll do well." "I *remember* how well it went," is much more inspiring. These minor shifts in language cause major shifts in your subconscious mind. It helps remove any doubt and gives you a new freedom to believe in yourself and your work.

Remember to be in the moment, and enter the "jazz and remembering zone." You have to reach for the magic, knowing it's there and inviting it in. While the steps to get there are described in words, you can really get flying when you realize that it's all yours. You can find your own way into the zone and take notes only as a leaping-off point. And although jazz can be taught as a method, it's the ingredients that are important to study. Remembering is like this, too.

The "Ingredients" of the Remembering Process

- 1 part visualization
- 1 part clearing the field of blocks and ego
- 1 part playful openness
- 1 part faith in the unity of all things
- 1 part belief in unified time

These ingredients allow a "crossing over" from your immediate reality to a world where you can invent your future. The mind tunes itself to the place of co-creation and the details compound themselves, starting as small clues, then gaining steam as callings, memories, and finally, as realities.

The first wave of efficacy is seeing the possibility of overwhelming success. Sometimes just getting a glimpse of success, or what it would look and feel like, pushes through the resistance and opens up ideas that didn't exist previously. For example, when I started contemplating writing this book, imagining a million dollars in sales allowed a certain part of me to dream big. Seeing yourself winning a fight or a race, or achieving any other goal is a common visualization technique. It's giving that vision a feeling of "remembering" that stimulates other emotions and idea potential that mere visualization won't do.

Like with jazz, you collect the pieces, walk in that direction, and watch for clues as to how to speak the language. Just as jazz has a language all of its own, so does the Remembering Process, but remembering is far easier. Simply bring your openness and your imagination. Universal time will then create the visualization, a film in your mind, of what you did to get to where you got. Perhaps for you, you will notice a scent or have a flash of insight. Trust what your future self sends you and develop it.

Words in conversation do hold weight, but it's your feelings within and the environment you create that really carries the power. The Remembering Process allows you to enhance and expand both.

A friend of mine who had to give a talk to a group of businesspeople was nervous and asked for my advice.

I said, "Why not try the Remembering Process?"

"What's that?" she asked.

"Basically, you go mentally into the future, past your talk, and try to remember how it went," I explained. "Just imagine it's over, and you're recalling how you did."

I could sense she wasn't sure how the process worked, so I added some coaching.

"Okay, let's pretend it's next Monday," I began. "Your presentation is over. It was days ago. It's now a memory. Tell me how your talk went."

She smiled. "It went great."

"Tell me about it."

"I don't remember all the details now, but I recall that I was calm. Everyone was attentive. I know I laughed a lot and gave great information. They wanted my website and business card afterward. I had a really good time. I don't remember it all, but I know it went better than I expected."

"Sounds like a great talk to me," I chimed in. "What else?"

She wasn't sure how to reply.

I added, "This is your memory, so you're free to recall it in any way you wish. You're creating the event as you remember it. How do you want to remember it?"

"As something great," she replied.

"Here's your chance!"

"Well, I think I told memorable stories, the mood was light and playful, and the audience members were engaged and asked many questions. It was a hit."

"Excellent. How do you feel about your talk now?"

"I'm ready!"

And yes, she went out a few days later and gave a terrific presentation.

— Joe

Details Matter

The more details you can infuse into the Remembering Process, the better. This is what makes a memory come alive and brings rich-feeling tones and emotions.

Imagine biting into a lemon, and you'll know what I mean. Imagine the impact of the lemon juice, the almost burning sensation on your lips, and how the sweetness is walloped by the tart explosion in your mouth. Is your mouth watering?

When you're practicing the Remembering Process, try to recall the music you were listening to when you found out your book was published, or when a new client accepted your offer. Where were you? Were you listening at home, in the car, or on the go with earbuds?

Here's a good starting point: "Remember" what you were reading when you started to create your life and destiny using the Remembering Process. What shoes were you wearing? Did you change toothpaste? Did you break off that toxic relationship? Did you start taking walks every day?

Use all of your senses, especially ones you aren't as aware of normally, such as your sense of smell. Scents trigger memories. For example, when you reached your fitness goals, do you remember the scents in your kitchen? Did you have to switch deodorants because you were working out so much that you needed stronger odor protection? Did you wash your Vibram FiveFingers running shoes a lot because they stunk from sweat? Did you have Odor-Eaters in your Adidas? Get vivid.

Memories hold such power, both positive and negative. The good ones make us feel nostalgic; the bad ones can get us stuck. Can you remember the first thing you did when you realized that you would never be held back by the past in the same way again?

With any memory, respect the imperfection of it and allow for changes, additions, and subtractions. Vagueness allows for movement, whereas traditional intention and manifestation techniques often have a tendency toward tightness around our desires. The Remembering Process allows for haziness—or wiggle room—for other, even better and truer, realities to come forth.

It reminds me of the method that Frank Gehry, a Los Angeles–based architect, uses when he begins a building project. He starts with a form of gesturing that looks like Pigpen from the Peanuts cartoon. When Frank is drawing, he does these scribbles that turn into massive, stunning buildings with curves that no one else does.

That's what we're looking for here at first—scribbles and gestures of our true life.

At its heart, there is a kind of massaging of peripheral feelings and intangible drivers. You keep working on figuring out the overall feel and the attainable details until you've drawn a more accurate picture of what you really want. Along the way, you can scratch out the details that don't look right and add the ones that feel better.

Guidelines for the Remembering Process

- Do your best to relax.

- Bring your most playful self.

- Decide if you feel that you are participating in the process from an earthly brainstorm or the unified state. Either way is perfectly acceptable, but it's good to define where you stand.

Are you using this as a logical way to brainstorm, or as a way of connecting with the Divine? If you're willing to take the leap of faith into telling yourself that these things are your destiny and that they're part of your spiritual purpose, you may get more joy and enlightenment out of the process . . . but only if you're comfortable with it. If you feel uncomfortable with it, then use the process as a game—a fun technique to help you tap into your creativity. You don't have to stay in one mode or the other forever; you can try both.

- Start remembering the desired result.

- Begin with the big results and then play with smaller details like wispy dreams. *I got the promotion! I wore my blue suit that day. I ate potato pancakes for breakfast, and my boss smiled at me as soon as I walked in the door.*

- Follow the path of your thoughts and visions. Go with the feelings and memories that feel most like they happened. Dream out loud. Remember what you did in more recent times to get to that future now.

- You may want to record the session or write it out.

- As you remember the same result for a number of days in a row, clarity about how you got there occurs. If I asked you to talk about your experiences in third grade for four days straight, the fourth day is likely to possess more detail than the first.

- Keep in mind that the moment you begin to "want" this to happen, you're no longer in the Remembering Process; instead, you'll be thinking it's possible that it didn't happen. This disconnects you from the desired outcome.

Start with a Desire

The order of flow in the Remembering Process is simple and basic.

Want it—this is the first sketch. Then remember you have it.

Our desires, those things we think we "want," are our cosmic memory waking back up. I want to write a song and then I start remembering that this song exists. I want that Ferrari, but then I realize that it's already mine.

I remember my first Ferrari with such pleasure and nostalgia. I had chosen that target because it's such a distinct and charged archetype in my mind, as well as in the collective mind. Also, as I began the path toward remembering my beloved black Ferrari, I was so far from having the financial means to buy one that to own one would prove a certain facet of reality for me. It's a perfect symbol of the pure potential that exists in the unified plane.

I can remember my car's wonderful tires. I connected with the designers at Pininfarina, the Ferrari design center. The car speaks and embodies another

way of thinking, seeing, and living in reality, moving
from where you are to where you want to be.

Our desires are like little homing signals from the universe. They are calling us home to our ability to create just like the Creator archetypes in all of our favorite religions.

So we begin by saying that we want something and eventually change the word *want* to *remember.* The interesting part is that many people get stuck at the first step; they have no idea what they want. Often, insecurity and fear will keep us from being clear about living our best lives. We have a fear of past failures, an unnatural push to the future, and an antipathy to uncomfortable-feeling states in the present moment.

Quick journaling and sketching is a great way to free yourself for the creative process, allowing a timeless wisdom to flow. Many great teachers have espoused stream-of-consciousness writing, or something like it. Natalie Goldberg, author of the highly influential book *Writing Down the Bones*, encourages her students to write whatever comes out. Specifically, she suggests writing with pen and paper (not typing) for ten minutes without ever letting your hand stop moving—that means you don't pick your hand up while you think about what to write next. You just keep the pen moving. You don't edit anything out because that leaves room for the inner critic to take hold. Your objective isn't to write brilliantly, but just to get limbered up and see what streams forth. It can be brilliant, or it can be utter crap. She says that if enough crap piles up, a flower will eventually spring from the fertilized creative ground. I had the honor of studying with Natalie, and this permission was a key to the rest of my creative life. It could be yours, too.

The following exercise can help you unblock and expand your own creativity.

> Try this: Set a timer, and write in your journal for ten minutes. Don't stop writing or cross words out. Don't read what you wrote. Start remembering your future. Remember the details—smell them, taste them.
>
> - Don't say: "I want a Ferrari."
>   Say: *I remember the smell of the tires.*
>
> - Don't say: "I want a happy, healthy family." Say: *I remember the smell of the newborn baby's beautiful, reddish skin.*
>
> - Don't say: "I'll try to write a song."
>   Say: *I remember the texture of the shrink-wrap as I was opening my new CD.*
>
> - Don't say: "I want to be a successful musician." Say: *I remember the feel of my blazer and my boots as I walked into the Grammy ceremonies. I remember the sun and the haze of the Los Angeles air.*

Once you have a desire in mind, it's time to put the Remembering Process into action to help you attain it. As I mentioned earlier, it's a simple six-step process that you can work on right now.

The Remembering Process in Six Easy Steps

Step 1: Relax

Access to bigger wisdom—states of transformation and growth—begins with relaxation. Choosing when to do a Remembering Process session is one of the most important predictors of its success, and it hinges around one thing: how relaxed you are (or aren't) at the time.

One of the best times to do this is first thing in the morning, just after you've awakened and before your internal critic has become fully alert. You know that critic—the one who likes to tell you that your dreams are silly and that you can't do it. Luckily, he's pretty groggy first thing in the morning, so it's great if you can start remembering before he can interrupt.

Starting the process before you've spoken to anyone can be very effective. When you start speaking, checking e-mails and texts, and getting into your general day, your social self has to wake up. Many artists advocate a morning writing practice for the same reason. Once your ego wakes up and you start doing various roles and jobs, doubt and self-consciousness can arise along with the critic.

Here are other ways to access a relaxed state, too:

Meditate. If you don't already know how to get into a meditative state, you may want to try listening to a guided-imagery CD—there are lots of them available on iTunes and Amazon.com if you search for "guided imagery" or "guided meditation." Or you can simply put on relaxing instrumental music, sit or lie down comfortably, and focus on a simple focal point—a lit candle works well for this purpose—while you allow your mind to clear.

Spend time alone in nature. Take a long walk or hike. This is its own form of meditation. Nature has its own calendar. It's best to be alone for this because—even if you're with someone special—another's presence will color your perceptions.

Use guided-relaxation techniques. During guided relaxation, you first tense and then relax each of your muscle groups, helping you become aware of your body's tensions so you can let them go. There are many scripts and recordings that can help you, or you can simply start at the top of your body (forehead, eyes, ears), and work your way down to your toes. Clench the muscles for five seconds, then relax the muscles, and then move to the next area.

Focus on your breathing. For a quick way to relax, simply take a few minutes to do nothing but focus on breathing in and out. You want your exhalation to be longer than your inhalation, like long sighs. Try inhaling to the count of four, holding to the count of four, and then exhaling to the count of eight. Just keep repeating this until you feel calm and grounded.

Pick your pleasure. Take a bath or a long shower. Drink herbal tea. Have someone rub your shoulders or feet. Stretch. Color with crayons. Listen to a "sounds of nature" CD. There is no wrong way to relax—find whatever you enjoy, and start there.

Keep in mind that your process doesn't have to be perfect. Just allow yourself to become more calm, quiet, and relaxed than you were. You can soon "remember" how you got more and more relaxed.

Find a quiet place where you can be alone. Sit comfortably in a meditative and grounded posture. Breathe and relax for a minute or two. Be very present to this Newtonian moment.

Step 2: Agree with the Present Moment

Agreeing with the present moment is quite possibly the linchpin of the Remembering Process.

I consciously agree that *I am here now*—that whatever it is I am remembering into my life had this exact moment as a part of its life. So often we are trying to bend life away from what it is right now. Fully embracing this moment is requisite to arriving at any other and allows the soft flow of time.

There is *now*, as we know it.

This is it.

Before you can climb aboard alternate realities or change this reality, you must agree with the current one. Tell yourself, *I am here now, and this is where I'm meant to be. This is a necessary step on my path, and I will enjoy it and work in harmony with it. I do not need to rush away from here. I am always in the right place at the right time.*

Step 3: Play, Trust, and Observe

Start to play with the process as a fascinated observer, like a bird-watcher.

The human mind *loves* to play with space, time, and reality. You're going to a place that you might not have visited since you were very young. Remember when it was easy to just make up stories? When you played "pretend" with your friends, inventing plots about saving sick animals, traveling to outer space, or hanging out with imaginary friends? Remember how real those imaginary experiences felt?

As we get older, we forget how to play with our imagination. We stop inventing these wonderful stories, and we're told to live in "reality" and learn that 2 + 2 = 4 and that grass is green, not purple. But what if we could erase all that teaching and just allow our mind the freedom to believe whatever it wants to believe again, at least for a little while?

In your relaxed and accepting state, allow your mind to ruminate about whatever it is that you're trying to accomplish, and trust the images it gives you. If it helps, keep a pen and paper handy to doodle or write.

This step is, essentially, inspired brainstorming, allowing you to tap into a deeper state of relaxed observing. For now, let your brain imagine, scan, or search for clues to the next level. Maintain that playful state, and trust what you see.

I spoke at a Hay House "I Can Do It!" event in Austin in 2013 and revealed an imagery method that I think you'll love. It can help you fully understand the Remembering Process so that you can use it right now, in real time. In essence, you get to use your imagination to playfully move into actual unified time. Here's how it works:

Onstage during my talk, I explained that scientists keep discovering new planets, and one of the newly discovered planets has life on it. When the scientists looked more closely, they realized that the planet was identical to ours.

In other words, the planet they discovered was another Earth. It contained the same ratio of oxygen, the same continents, the same atmosphere, and even the same people. That meant that on this "Other Earth," there is another you, who is identical in looks, temperament, genes, lifestyle, and more.

But there was one key difference.

On this Other Earth, time was six months ahead. That meant that everything you're worried about right now was already resolved on Other Earth. The future you had already found a solution or resolution. The things you wanted to take place already happened.

I went on to tell the audience that this was good news for you. All you have to do is visit with the future you and ask how you got what you wanted or solved what the issues were. I jokingly said that Richard Branson was establishing a global airline and taking passengers to the Other Earth, but that you could also Skype the future you and ask yourself to remember how you handled what you're currently wrestling with.

You can do this right now, with your mind. All you have to do is play along. Pretend this other planet is real. (Who's to say it isn't?) Pretend there's a future you, and you can contact yourself. Do it right now.

Simply close your eyes, and let a dialogue unfold in your mind. There's no right or wrong way to do it. You're just having fun, letting creativity lead the way. Ask the future you questions, and let the answers come.

If it's easier, write down your experience. It might look like this:

Me: How did I finally attract the perfect relationship?

Future Me: It was easy once you quit trying so hard and focused on being happy with yourself.

The main idea here is to let the "future you" remember how you solved the concerns or issues that the present you has. Then see how the advice sits with you.

This little exercise will expand your mind and help you realize that the future you and the present you are on the same time line. By visiting the future you on this "Other Earth," you tap into your own creativity—six months from now, where all your current problems and desires have already been handled.

— Joe

You must be prepared for randomness. Whatever comes to your mind, be open and trust it. There may be nonsense—trust it. You may get immediate and direct wisdom that speaks for itself.

I suggest journaling or drawing what your inner guide is trying to speak to you about. You can also try mind-mapping, a technique where you draw diagrams about your thoughts. Your central idea goes in the middle, and then you draw branches to write out your associated thoughts, going deeper into the ones that feel the most promising by drawing more "twigs" off those branches with your further thoughts. You can find examples of this at www.mindmapping.com. Over time, you will get sharper and faster at finding the useful messages and images and expanding on them.

Once you start seeing the reality "as if" it happened, you will start to open up to its clear potential reality. Later, when we leap ahead, you may have the blessing of realizing that it actually *did* happen in time and space; and a deeper, calmer belief and confidence will set in. For now, merely being able to see the "imaginable" reality will create a sense of possibility that no other model I've tried will.

Step 4: Use Touchstones

Instead of just relying on your imagination to supply all the details, provide yourself with physical clues to keep yourself in the right frame of mind. Like Joe did when he had a designer put his image on the cover of *Rolling Stone,* give yourself things to look at and touch throughout your day that remind you of what you're "remembering." Make it real.

In 1990, while he was still a struggling, unknown comic actor, Jim Carrey wrote himself a check for $10 million. In the memo line, he added, "For acting services rendered," and he postdated the check for five years later. What Jim was doing subconsciously was using the Remembering Process—he was traveling into the future and remembering that he had been paid $10 million for acting, and now he was coming back to the present to remind himself of that fact. He carried that check around in his wallet, and by 1995, five years since he'd written that check, he had far surpassed those earnings. He'd starred in numerous blockbusters, and his going rate had soared to $20 million per film.

The check was his tangible evidence that what he remembered was real. What can you do to show yourself the same thing? Get creative—if you want to remember that you own the house of your dreams, take a picture of yourself in front of it. Start browsing around online or in person for the decor and fixtures. Draw up what your landscaping looks like. Pick up "change of address" forms at the post office. Start shopping and getting your hair cut in the town you're going to live in.

If your desired outcome is to win an Academy Award, pick out the dress or tuxedo you wore to the event. Write your acceptance speech. Collect photos of how you remember wearing your hair. Do whatever you can to collect evidence that your memory is real.

It's along the lines of creating a vision board—a poster board with images of things you're hoping to manifest in your life—but with an important distinction: I want you to put *you* into the picture. In other words, don't just hang up pictures of your ideal car. Actually go and test-drive it and have someone take a picture of you in it. Don't just clip out the words "*New York Times* Bestseller List." Type up the list with the name of your book at the top. Personalize it as much as you can to show your mind that you don't just "want" these things; you have these things. You have accomplished your dreams at some point in the future, and you have proof.

Step 5: Leap into Quantum Remembering
—the Unified State

"I lose myself at some point during almost every musical performance. There's some point of struggle and super self-consciousness, but I always get lost at some point. While I'm playing, there's a pattern of struggling through something and then cracking through it by a weird combination of willpower and letting go. That's the most enjoyable thing for me: 'Uh oh, he's gone!'"

— David Torn, Grammy Award–winning artist

This is an optional step, but if you're inclined, this is where you'll hop on board the Cosmic Quantum Express and open yourself to a unified and connected plane of existence—where every song you'll ever write is written, every book and its sequel completed, and everything you'll ever say is already said somewhere in time.

While you don't have to worry about your inner skeptic, keep in mind that sometimes your ego and nervous system may be too active and agitated to allow you to slip, skip, or step into this dimension. This is a step off of the earth—"out of your mind" and into a different reality. The current moment becomes perfect, as it should be, since you remember it as a step along the way to your ultimate destiny. When you step into this plane, it just is.

There's a great meditation book called *Don't Just Do Something, Sit There,* and that title exemplifies what I mean. Sometimes, it's about *being* instead of *doing.* Of course you have to find the right balance of both, but many people spend their lives doing, doing, doing, and forget to find time to just be. It's hard to connect to the Divine Creator within you if you never take the time to search for it.

You don't have to "make" yourself do anything to get to the unified state; you just have to allow yourself the room to believe. It's a matter of finding enough relaxation and faith to gratefully touch the Divine aspect within you. Try saying this to yourself:

This is my perfect moment. It is exactly where I am meant to be right now. My past, present, and future are all connected; and I feel confident knowing that I have already achieved everything I want to somewhere on this plane of existence. I am living my best life, and I remember that I have everything I need and everything I want. There is nothing left for me to want, because I already have it. I am the only person who can live my best life; and I live it with trust, love, openness, and creativity. I relinquish my fear and anxieties about the future. Good things are coming my way every day.

Step 6: Collect the Wisps

If you're waiting for the entire creative project or resolution to come out fully formed during the Remembering Process, you may be frustrated. It *can* work that way, but more often, you'll find that all you get are little flashes of something-or-other. An image, a few words, a little melody.

As soon as you start thinking that you have to remember things the right way, you may block the information that comes in because you're afraid of getting it wrong. Instead, acknowledge and appreciate any little bit that comes your way in these sessions, and use them as jumping-off points, like brainstorming.

Keep in mind that you'll still have to do the work. If you're trying to "remember" writing a book, and you get a few great thoughts about what might go in it, don't keep waiting for more, which is really just stalling. Collect those wisps and start writing! You can continue the Remembering Process throughout—every night, if you want, to "remember" what you're going to write the next day. You'll probably find that it gets easier and easier to put the process to work the more regularly you do it. But don't get so caught up in the heady stuff that you fail to actually use the information you're given, or you're just going to be left with a bunch of fun "memories" and nothing to show for it.

Practicing the Remembering Process

Here are some exercises to help you tap into your higher self and start thinking in a future mind-set. In order to receive the most significant gains from the following exercises, get into the most relaxed and comfortable state possible. Practice the guidelines from earlier in the chapter. Just doing these exercises will have a positive effect on your thinking. If you take these to the level of prayer or communion with a higher power, they can help draw your best outcomes with far greater power.

Positivity and joy are the key ingredients. These are the optimal states to connect with your dreams. The magic of remembering your feats as already accomplished is that doubt gets erased, which ultimately allows the task to be completed with relative ease. It's the doubt and fear of failure that stops so many worthwhile endeavors before they can get out of the gate.

Conduct a Grave Remembering

"Here lies Daniel Barrett. Husband, father, friend, artist, producer, author, entrepreneur, and philanthropist."

As shocking as it may be, one way to engage the Remembering Process is to go to your own funeral. This exercise isn't for everyone, as it can be upsetting or unsettling. Sometimes, however, that's just what you need to wake up to your highest self. Writing your own eulogy allows you to honor your life as you have created it. You can look back on this moment from the perspective of your whole tenure on Earth.

The year Daniel's first child was born was a series of revelations about connection, motivation, and intention. The projects he started that year not only provided well for his family, but they also served a wide number of people in his community and beyond. His healthy, wealthy, and happy lifestyle was a light to those around him and those afar.

You can be extremely detailed about whatever you are currently seeking to manifest. In this exercise, explain in detail how you achieved and overcame these challenges to fulfill your dreams. Just the act of writing about yourself in the reverential and loving tone of a eulogy will fill your heart with positive energy. As you would for a respected loved one, write and rewrite this tribute until it's clear and specific. Remember all the way back to this calendar year, and describe how you saw through whatever you needed to in order to achieve your goals.

Write a Diary Entry from the Future

Date your journal for the future. If the eulogy exercise feels grim or a little too intense, feel free to just write one or a series of journal entries about your "future past." Be descriptive about the details of your intelligent decision making and problem solving.

As you write, know that it's common for part of your brain to chime in with doubts. Stay with the memories of your success. You have to go out on the limb with yourself, suspend disbelief, and really play.

Draft a Letter of Congratulations

Go to www.futureme.org, and write yourself a glowing letter of congratulations for your accomplishments. Include all the juicy details about how you made it happen, rejecting the Upper-Limit Problem that could have held you back from breaking through to even higher heights than you'd originally imagined. Describe the inner characteristics that gave you the strength and direction to achieve your desired outcomes. Here's what mine looks like:

> *Dear Future Me,*
>
> *I am so, so proud of you. It has been quite the year!*
> *I hope you are resting well. You deserve it.*
> *Congrats on your beautiful baby. Watching you take on the role of father is moving. You are loving, gentle, present, and responsible. Things were sweet with Andi, but now it's at a whole new level of connection. The joy of family surrounds you.*

It was expected that you would take Rubicon Artist Development to the next level. Nobody could foresee the major leaps in profit, enrollment, artist success and satisfaction, and overall operations. You've become a major player in the Austin music and business scenes. Your attention to detail helped create the strategic partnerships necessary to move forward like this. Your positive outlook drew the best and brightest to your team.

When you add the success of <u>The Remembering Process</u> to that, it makes this year stand out among all others to this point. Your finances are looking phenomenal, and you are wisely investing some of that major surplus into real estate in Austin. Being an excellent money manager allowed even more abundance to flow your way.

Congratulations on the discipline and work flow you have created for yourself. It's a pleasure to watch the details of your life be handled so well. It looks so effortless, and I am sure it feels wonderful.

Finally, among all of that, your health has been so strong. Your athleticism and energy level are at an all-time high. Watching you do those pull-ups is a thrill since they were on your goals list for so long.

I tip my hat to you. Well done!

With love from your best friend,
Me

Create a Magazine Article

Write a magazine article, record, podcast, or radio segment describing your accomplishments. Just like Jim Carrey carried around that $10 million check he'd written to himself, put something in writing that will help you envision your best future. If you're feeling a little shy about the previous exercises, this one may help you "brag" because it's written from the perspective of a third party. The news article would focus on three to five of the most important factors in your success. In this exercise, be more concise and generally describe how you made it happen. Once again, pour on the meaningful praise for what you've achieved!

When Not to Use the Remembering Process

While Steps 1 through 4 are available as thinking and problem-solving tools at any time, crossing over into Step 5 ("Leap into Quantum Remembering") requires that you become grounded in a calm, healthy place. If you're hungry, angry, lonely, or tired, it's very difficult to enter the unified field of time. The acronym HALT represents these states, and it's often used when discussing recovery from an addiction.

Eating well for your body type and activity level allows your body and brain to function properly and can help keep your emotions in check. Anger puts you in a defensive and closed mental position, activating your "lizard brain"— the prehistoric brain that only wants to fight or flee. While it's certainly human and normal to be angry from time to time, you need to use earthly means to express and process this emotion before accessing the higher circuitry that's available.

The remembering technique is about opening up, being vulnerable in seeking your highest life and self, and letting go of dualistic thinking. *Duality* refers to any kind of "either/or" thinking. In this case, it closes off options and tightens your approach in a negative way. Thinking that your desires are "either/or" sounds like: "I want to pursue my passions, but I want to have financial security." The two can be joined, of course. Just replace the *but* with *and:* "I want to pursue my passions, *and* I want to have financial security."

If you're lonely, it's important to reach out to others. A certain level of connection by simple, earthly means is essential to a happy mind-set. If you're lonely and having a hard time drawing positive people to you, using the first three steps of the process can help you create healthy connections.

Finally, getting ample rest also helps keep your brain and body healthy, allowing a graceful, easier transition into an open and unified state. Again, you can use Steps 1 through 4 to easily create and "remember" a life that has a healthy balance of rest and rejuvenation.

If you're struggling, consider whether therapy would offer you benefits. I go to therapy once a week and have done so for a number of years. I have a happy life, plenty of friends, and the woman of my dreams. I'm blessed to live with plenty of money for necessities *and* playful wants. I thoroughly love my life. The reason I see a therapist regularly is to keep my brain functioning in its highest, most peaceful, and aware state possible. I have a sensitive disposition, like that Ferrari I love so much that is in my field somewhere.

A high-performance vehicle often needs some consistent and adept tuning up. If you put yourself in a crisis state, you stress your brain too much to be receptive to the more subtle energies of the cosmos. In unified consciousness, there is nothing inherently wrong with that, but why work that way when you're just as capable of working in a more advanced, joyful, and satisfying way—and of using your thought energy to travel on to your highest destiny?

The Remembering Process-able part of your brain is knocked out of receptivity with any sort of fight-or-flight reactivity. You immediately lower down, losing access to your higher self. It doesn't work if you have an emotional trigger because the trigger implies a dualistic thinking pattern.

Dear Dan,

I remember a better intention when singing.

I recall sitting down with you and explaining how my mind works so that I could better express myself as a singer. I think this helped you with all your clients. You would sometimes ask me to pause and reflect on the feeling I wanted to communicate before singing a song. Every time I did that, it messed up my timing and made me feel "off." From there I couldn't enjoy my playing. I felt disconnected, which was the opposite of what you wanted me to feel. I kept reflecting on that until I realized that there was an erroneous underlying assumption.

In short, people don't have feelings first—they have thoughts first.

People often think that the feelings come first, but everything from cognitive psychology to the Emotional Freedom Techniques (EFT) and Thought Field Therapy (TFT) prove otherwise. It's the thoughts that create the feelings.

I remember that when I would consider the thought I wanted to convey to a listener, then and only then could I let whatever feelings arise in me while playing to help deliver it. And as a self-help singer/songwriter, the thought or message is far more important than any feeling I have. In other words, I can't control what people feel or even receive, but I can focus on my clear intent and let it act as a seed I offer to others through sound.

I remember that this insight shifted my performing. Instead of trying to focus on feeling first, which disconnected me and dropped my energy and joy, I instead concentrated on the message/thought/intention that I consciously wanted to deliver, and then allowed myself to deliver it while trusting the listeners to receive what was right for them.

I remember you reflected on this, and it opened up a whole new world of possibilities for you in your coaching, including being more flexible with your clients' different styles.

Since I'm remembering all this, I could have some parts fuzzy . . .

— Joe

When clients have an unresolved issue they're dealing with, I often recommend they "tap" using an emotional clearing technique known as EFT, a process that Joe and many others have written extensively about. EFT stands for "Emotional Freedom Techniques," and it's a combination of acupressure and positive affirmations. You tap specific areas of your head and chest while you think about the issue and also say positive affirmations aloud for dealing with it. The combination of the two things can help to clear your psychological blocks.

For example, I was triggered with emotions of anger and hurt one weekend and was having a difficult time writing. I tapped as I said, *Even though I am too upset to write, I deeply and completely forgive myself.* As I repeated this, I began to feel on track and able to get back into the writing.

If you want to learn more about EFT, visit www .garythink.com or www.eftuniverse.com. There are also YouTube videos on the subject that you can watch to see the technique demonstrated.

My intention here is to let you know that there are times when you may not be able to devote your attention to the Remembering Process, and that's okay. There have been times when I couldn't get relaxed or focused enough to find the right vibe for it, either—mostly when I've been hungry, angry, lonely, or tired. When you have other pressing physical or emotional needs that haven't been met, you're in a compromised state where it will be difficult to get much of anything else done. Resolve what needs resolving first, and then try the process again.

We live in a human "animal" body and must honor and tend to its emotions and needs. It is, after all, our time machine.

You've now learned the steps to use so you can put the Remembering Process into action in your life. There are two ways to approach it, though: belief mode and nonbelief mode. If you're at all skeptical about the process, read on. I'll address how it works regardless of whether or not you're a "true believer."

BELIEVE IT OR NOT

"Our normal waking consciousness, rational consciousness as we call it, is but one special type of consciousness, whilst all about it, parted from it by the flimsiest of screens, there lie potential forms of consciousness entirely different. . . . No account of the universe in its totality can be final, which leaves these other forms of consciousness quite disregarded."

—William James

There is elegance to the Remembering Process, regardless of which category—believer or non—you fall into. As a mental sharpening tool, you can use it for all types of creative or logical thinking capacities, such as brainstorming, writing, and social skills. You can win a chess match, land a sale, or write a short story from a relaxed, inspired, and confident state of possibility.

In other words, you don't have to believe in the metaphysical component to receive its many gifts. The technique immediately and automatically scaffolds to your present level of belief and openness. And if you are ready and willing, it will allow you to play with the very fabric of time and reality to co-create with the universal life force. The beauty of the Remembering Process is that it works on multiple levels. Each step is productive on its own.

You now know that the first step is simply relaxing. As you do that right now, it's already a win. Every great practice requires this, and there are so many ways to do it. Having some kind of meditation practice, whether it's a Buddhist sitting practice or puffing cigars on the back porch, is key. It doesn't matter what it is as long as it slows your heartbeat and clears your mind.

The simple attempt of relaxing into these places, knowing that during a portion of this time you can have an inspired experience, can be enough to create the changes you're looking for—even if you don't believe in concepts like unified time and truly remembering the future.

> The Remembering Process can be used for anything—deep spiritual questions and small, practical problems alike.
>
> One day I was frustrated that my computer wasn't working, and I had a lot of work to do. I felt my hands were tied. When I shared my predicament with Daniel, he said, "I remember it all worked out, and you got your computer up and running. I don't recall when or how, but I know it was handled."
>
> His words eased me. It reminded me that in the future, my computer would no doubt be fixed. It didn't matter whether I really believed he could see

into my future or whether I believed he was making a reassuring guess, and I chose to go along with his thought. In either case, it dissolved my stress.

It's important to realize that my computer still wasn't fixed in that moment. But remembering that it was allowed me to relax. After all, the stress wasn't fixing the machine *at all*. When stress is gone, answers are easier to see.

And, of course, that machine now works. I'm writing these words to you on it.

— Joe

Nonbelief Mode

If you don't believe in gravity in this earthly plane, you can still participate in its laws (nonbelief mode). Gravity's feelings are not hurt, but you may find yourself barking up the wrong trees and pushing stones uphill. Yet if you truly believe that gravity is in action upon your body, you can play the games of balance and motion with joy. You can work in harmony versus applying effort and strain.

It's the same with the Remembering Process, so if achieving a unified state of consciousness seems far out, that's fine. Certainly not everyone will be interested in it, nor believe or care about it. If you think that is too much to believe right now, the Remembering Process can still open up parts of the brain that you don't have working on a current challenge or task. It can also strengthen your intuition, or psychic abilities, which you are probably in tune with if you're on a spiritual path; although if you aren't, or don't have those feelings with some frequency, this could feel like a stretch.

No matter your level of interest, developing your "remembering" faculties can strengthen your mind's neural connections and also the circuitry that crosses into the universal *now*. As Einstein said, you can't solve a problem with the same kind of thinking that created it. In order to change your overall way of thinking, it requires several smaller changes first—changes in the "default" neural pathways in your brain, otherwise known as your habits.

Let's say you usually deal with stress by drinking alcohol, but you want to learn a healthier way to handle your problems. You've decided to take up yoga and meditation. From the first day you decide to make this change, you intend to make it wholeheartedly; however, your brain may need more finessing. It's currently hardwired to go down a particular path—the one you've trained it to associate with stress. Your brain thinks, *Stress means I should drink alcohol.* The neural pathway between stress and alcohol is strong and difficult to break. However, it can clearly be done. It just means retraining your brain through your thoughts and actions.

So now you intentionally go into a meditative state or practice yoga when you feel stressed, even when your brain is telling you that it's time for alcohol. Eventually, it becomes second nature—the "Stress = alcohol" pathway gets weaker, and the "Stress = yoga" pathway grows stronger until it becomes the default.

The Remembering Process works in the same way—the more you do it, the more you strengthen its connections to problem solving. At first, it may feel weird and unnatural, and you'll probably be inclined to face your problems in the same manner that you always have before. (Obviously, it's not an ideal manner, or you wouldn't be interested in learning about other methods.) But the more often you do it, the more your brain gets trained to go down that pathway. It becomes more automatic; instead of grumbling about your problems to co-workers, you will think, *Hmm, maybe I can "remember" a solution to this problem.*

It's not limited to the Remembering Process, but open to many different creative methods—and I suggest that you try out as many as you can. When you're faced with a problem, it's great if you can look at it through multiple lenses, trying on various ways of dealing with it. The effect of playing around with your creativity like this can change the way you perceive the challenges in your life and make you feel more empowered to live the life you want. Just by doing Steps 1 to 4 of the Remembering Process, you'll be on your way to better results in your life.

You don't need to believe in anything other than the here-and-now, and you can view it as an imagination game, just like you did in kindergarten when your teacher said, "Let's take a trip to the moon!" or "Let's go on an African safari today." You didn't furrow your brow then and say, "Wait, we're not *really* going to the moon." You played along. So give yourself permission to do that again—just play along, ignoring the cynical part that says this whole "remembering the future" thing is kind of crazy. Maybe it is. Who cares? If you think the notion that time is malleable and that we can play with it, á la *Back to the Future*, is crazy, then I give you permission to embrace this:

> *Daniel Barrett is a weirdo, and I don't believe all this stuff about traveling into the future and remembering things that haven't happened yet. But I'm going to play along only because it's a fun exercise*

*and a way to tap into my imagination. I may dream
up some cool stuff. I'm probably a weirdo in my own
way, too. So there.*

Having been to music school, I know many students
who learned only the nuts and bolts and were still able
to create music that makes sense, sounds good, and feels
good. And, even in nonbelief mode, the Remembering
Process is a great reverse-engineering tool. You can do
what artist and coach Ann Rea says to do: "Back up into
your goals." Start with the end result—let's say, buying
a house—and figure out the practical steps it will take to
get there. What will you need? You'll need to show a certain amount of income to qualify for a mortgage, research
and look around at houses, hire an inspector, hire movers,
and so on. "Remember" these steps. Write them down. Be
aware of where you are in the process and what needs to
happen next.

The Remembering Process is a wonderful planning
tool. Even if this is not technically affecting the nature of
time, tapping into the part of you that can remember in
detail gives your brain a clear, believable homing signal to
carry you toward your dreams.

I do believe there is a spiritual order to things that the
Remembering Process accesses and other manifestation
techniques miss. However, even without that power, the
ignition quality of giving such rich images and sensations to
your psyche will bring you closer to your dreams.

Here's an exercise you may wish to try to help you "remember" how to reach those dreams.

Write your desired goal or outcome at the top or center of a piece of paper. I like mind-mapping, so I start in the center of the paper. Multiple colors of pencil or ink are sometimes nice, and crayons are fine to use, too.

Picture the desired result, and remember all of the steps that led up to it.

Then make a list of everything it would take to hit that goal and work out the plan. Sometimes, even though you already know what you need to do, putting it in writing can help you solidify your next steps and figure out where you are on the path to your goal. The simple act of writing signifies a level of commitment beyond just thinking or talking about something.

Belief Mode

In belief mode, you can enter the realm of unified time and space. There is only one moment, and that is *now*. *Now* has a broad range and depth of energy and experience.

The crux is that the part of the human brain that can access the time and space continuum is closely related to our "normal" function of remembering. By using the circuitry of the brain that is already designed to remember or recall things, this process allows you to tap into the fabric of Einsteinium quantum time and bring into your current perceived *now* that which you think you "want."

If you open up to the paradigm of quantum time and parallel universes, you can "remember" things into your current reality. In this state, it becomes impossible to want for things. We simply "remember" their place in our energy field, and that thing or occurrence vibrates into our current state. We are able to feel gratitude now because we have what we seek already. It's in our hands.

To help yourself open up to the idea, try playing with it first: Think to yourself, *What if this is true?* Faith is a gift you give yourself. It's not a "to do." It's a "to be." You don't have to force yourself to do anything in order to believe; just try affirming for yourself that it's okay to take the leap of faith. It's okay to be wrong. It's okay to believe in something for no good reason other than that it feels right and might be helpful to you. It can be productive to try on a new faith and see if it fits.

Skepticism Is Okay, Too

> *"Confusion is a word we have invented for*
> *an order which is not yet understood."*
>
> — Henry Miller

On the other hand, I love and appreciate skepticism. One of the missing links in the New Age/New Thought/ self-help movement is a welcoming of skeptics and naysayers. If these premises don't hold up to questioning, then how sturdy are they?

I believe deeply in the unified state and this take on the fabric of time. However, even if I'm dead wrong, it's still making my life better every day. People often scoff at stories of people responding well to placebos, as though they've been duped. I say, let's use all possible means of gaining peace and happiness, including any version of the placebo effect that we can get our minds on. What does it cost us, really?

Experimenting and doing different things alone can change your life for the better. Even if you only get a good laugh, you are winning. Before you know it, you can laugh your way into a unified mind and be tickled by the nature of reality itself.

Yakir Aharonov, an Israeli physicist specializing in quantum physics, has said, "The advantage of being a theoretical physicist is that you never have to worry about the cost of a thought experiment." What does it cost you to think differently, abstractly, and with great hope and belief? What does it cost you to try to fly (as long as you attempt to from the ground and not out a window)? Conversely, what are the costs of the same old thinking? What are the costs of doing what you've always done?

In a unified plane of energy, skepticism is the counterbalance to belief. It is not only welcomed, but it also has the same worth as belief. Same coin, other side. The most divisive forces in human history are the belief systems that don't lovingly invite and allow other thoughts, disagreements, and questions.

What about critics who might say that even the Remembering Process is deluding yourself?

My research in placebos—defined by the *Oxford Dictionary* as "a harmless pill, medicine, or procedure prescribed more for the psychological benefit to the patient than for any physiological effect"—confirms that when you believe in something, your belief tends to make it come true. There's even a scientific study that revealed that when many people with knee problems were led to believe they had knee surgery—but in fact did not have the surgery—they were just as likely to report pain relief as the individuals who actually received the knee surgery. (For more info, see www.science daily.com/releases/2002/07/020712075415.htm.) Likewise, there are even more recent studies showing that a placebo will work even when the patient knows it's a placebo. (See www.guardian.co.uk /science/2010/dec/22/placebo-effect-patients -sham-drug.)

This isn't news. I've known about the power of belief since the 1960s, when I first read Claude Bristol's masterpiece, *The Magic of Believing*. Your belief molds reality. Believe something is true about yourself or your world, and you'll tend to attract the circumstances to match it.

This works with negative beliefs as well. The "nocebo" is a negative expectation and will just as easily create a match to it. In other words, if you believe things will go wrong, or something will have a harmful effect, you will tend to attract that expectation. (See http://curezone.org/art/read.asp ?ID=142&db=1&C0=14.)

All of this is to say that your beliefs determine what you attract now and in the future. When you use the Remembering Process, you are stepping into a time line that hasn't occurred in this present reality—yet. But it potentially exists in the future. After all, the "reality" you see is viewed through your perceptions, and those perceptions are made from your beliefs.

If you've met me, heard me speak, viewed my pictures, or seen me on television or in movies, you know that I wear rings and beads. I believe some of it is for branding and some of it has real esoteric mojo in it, and I believe it helps me. In fact, whenever I speak in public, I wear a special gem made in part from the Gibeon meteorite. That meteorite is older than planet Earth and estimated to be about four billion years old. It's beautiful, and I can feel extra energy when I wear it. It was also a gift from my wife, Nerissa, a decade ago, so it has sentimental value.

What's most important about it? My belief in it.

That said, what's actually real? I'd rather believe in a magical universe and see my life blossom with miracles than walk through it fearing every turn of a leaf. Said another way, the placebo isn't real, but the placebo effect is. What you believe matters more than reality, as it filters reality so that you only see what you expect. When you "remember," you begin to see a possible new future. From there, you can create it.

That, to me, is the best form of "magical thinking."

— Joe

You can benefit from the Remembering Process no matter where you enter it, whether you see it as simply an exercise for your imagination or something more. There are many ways to put it into practice in your life, and next, we'll uncover some of its applications you may not have considered.

⊜ ⊜ ⊜

APPLYING THE REMEMBERING PROCESS

"The creation of something new is not accomplished by the intellect but by the play instinct acting from inner necessity."

— Carl Jung

The Remembering Process has broad applications and, in this chapter, I've selected some of the most frequent questions I've been asked over the years in working with my clients to further show how I've used the process and how they've used the process with positive results. I hope that it will answer your own questions as well and open your mind to new ways to use this technique.

One day I went to my session with Daniel, and he mentioned that we needed a drummer for our studio time. We were getting ready to record *Strut!*, my first album of my own songs. Daniel wasn't worried, as we live in the Austin area and musicians are everywhere, but the drummer he'd originally lined up had fallen out.

I remember reflecting on what was on the album in the future. By remembering it, I got the idea to ask the other Joe Vitale if he'd consider being part of my studio band. It was a long shot. The other Joe Vitale is a famous drummer. He's been in rock and roll for decades and has played for every rock legend from Neil Young to you-name-it. I had this feeling that he might actually be on my album. I wasn't sure, but I went for it and wrote to him. He stunned me by agreeing to do it! We worked out the details, and he flew in for the recording. Joe elevated my work to new heights. He brought so much energy and enthusiasm that it transformed the recording and me.

And it all came from remembering that he was already on the album.

— Joe

Q: How do you use the Remembering Process with clients?

Joe and I are a great example of using the Remembering Process as collaborators. Throughout this book, you can see glimpses of the kind of interactions we've had, both individually and together, for his music albums and this book. Here's a Remembering Letter I wrote to him at one point in our process:

> Dear Joe,
>
> I remember this first letter to you, and a warm feeling enters my face and chest. I am in the first night of a three-day writing spree. I seem to remember that you found a similar joy and power in seclusion.
>
> I remember the Grammy screen saver on my studio computer monitors. I was remembering a CD . . . I'm pretty sure that it was yours. I think it was called <u>Blue Healer.</u> Different blues rhythms and riffs, and improvisations of Austin's greatest blues musicians with a polished, smooth, hypnotic, healing chanting over it. Joe Vitale chants blues that "Heals, Feels, and Reveals."
>
> It could be a dream, or I might remember that the CD was the first of a few . . . and matched a magazine's message perfectly. It might have been the way to get the first CD done quickly, with joy and ease, while incubating the songwriting and guitar shredding that came later.
>
> I remember that you came to collect a certain kind of guitar. You became an expert of sorts on a certain brand, and bought a few of the same varietal. Or maybe I did . . . but there were a handful of Telecasters, Les Pauls, or Danelectros in the studio.
>
> The songwriting process you are in took a wonderful step forward . . . another unexpected "strut" toward your original sound. Any last doubts you may

have had evaporated, and you fully owned your place as a songwriting genius . . . genius being that you captured your true spirit. I think we recorded the next album rather quickly! Feeling pumped.

Does any of that ring a bell? I remember having compiled a bunch of stuff for the book into a readable collection. It was on the break from Rubicon seasons, so I stopped heaven and earth. I remember I got inspired that you stopped heaven and earth when it's time to receive a book, and this is very much about stopping time—controlling our time perception and making immense time for a certain thing!

I remember it led me to an easy and fun marathon of writing. I remember eating lots of cacao nibs and drinking lots of water. I remember that I became an author and that my identity always included "author" after that. I remember that I listened to our album of chant a lot and stood in awe of how well it came out. I remember that you and I deepened our friendship and working flow even further, making us both grateful for and amazed by the quality and ease of the output. I remember that I started to lose the extra bit of weight on my belly during this process. I remember that I became a step tangibly closer to my Ferrari. Not sure what it was, but it was palpable.

I remember that when all of this happened, I found a new level of calm that felt amazing . . . that I gave and served in a whole new way, and I loved it.

— Dan

Aside from writing letters like the above with clients, I also use the process extensively throughout our sessions together. I tend to introduce the idea on the first meeting before potential clients hire me, so they know what they're in for! It starts our working relationship on the right playful note. As they reveal their goals and obstacles, I begin "remembering" with them—*I remember that you got past your stage fright and began performing in public just as well as you do in private.* If a client doesn't get scared off by my methods, then I know we can use the process together.

Like when you work with an improv comedy troupe, agreement with one another is important. Saying, "I don't know what you're talking about," or "No, that didn't happen," shuts down the whole game. When you want to redirect where a conversation is going, you can say, "Yes, and . . ." rather than a flat "No." So one important rule is to play along with each other *and* play off each other.

I've also asked clients to write dialogues between their current selves and their future selves. For example, I might start out with: "Ask your future self everything you had to do to get what you've wanted." They can share that dialogue with me or keep it to themselves.

Q: What's a favorite story of yours using the Remembering Process in a field other than music?

There are so many applications for the Remembering Process, some having to do with creative pursuits and some more practical. My wife, Andi, and I used it when we were ready to move to a new home. Instead of the normal way of going about things—that is, "choosing" a house—we "remembered" the house we got. Andi remembered an open floor plan where she could see into the living room while she was cooking in the kitchen, and I remembered the more important details, like where we'd have a Ping-Pong table.

As a result of the time we spent thinking about all this, I could walk into a place and feel that "this is just not where we lived." It was different from being picky or having specific tastes. It was just that certain places didn't feel at all like *where we had lived.*

Once we walked into the house we now live in, we could feel the dinner parties. We could remember the stream and the greenbelt outside.

Simple, yes, but it was a completely different paradigm from making "choices."

It was a memory we set from the beginning that led us to the right home.

Q: Is there a way to use the Remembering Process to find a partner or soul mate?

For this question, we use the past and the future. If you want love, remember love.

Remember the Newtonian past, first by remembering times you felt most loved by a parent, a dog, a child, or a friend. It doesn't matter what it is; we're only ramping up at this point.

Remember the feeling. How many senses can you describe? What did the day feel like? What did you wear? What smells were in the air? Sharpen your memories and pick one moment in your traditional, linear past when you felt well loved. This will heighten your senses and start the karmic line of love in motion.

Like attracts like. Love attracts love. Remember when you were loved, and remember with all of your senses.

Remember touch. Remember smells. Remember songs. Now remember a time in the future when you were loved. Here's an example:

> *I remember we were so relaxed at a pool between workshop sessions. I remember you playing beautiful music on a beautiful guitar, with beautiful people listening. I vaguely remember some drinks. Were they smoothies? Piña coladas? I can taste the coconut, either way. There may have been some cigars around. I remember our great health, and our easygoing communication. Was there some sort of concert that night? I am not wishing; I am not hoping. I am remembering that this happened, and then remembering everything that I did leading up to it. I try to remember some of the thoughts and choices I made today, tomorrow, and this week that set those wheels in motion.*

Don't imagine. *Remember.*
Don't wish. *Remember.*
Next, find love in *this* current moment, as you know it. Joe found love in a pencil.

> My "pencil story" has become famous. You can see me tell it in the movie *The Compass.* In short, it goes like this:
> I had been living in poverty for a long time. But I kept working on myself, reading books from the library, going to free talks and events—doing my best to clean up my thinking and get out of the misery.

Along the way, I heard about gratitude. People told me that when you feel grateful, you change your inner state of being, and that in turn would change your outer life. Right. I was too smart for that con, so I resisted it. I said, "I'll feel grateful when I have something to feel grateful for!"

And as long as I stubbornly refused to give thanks, I stayed in the muck.

So one day I decided to try this "gratitude non-sense thing." I looked around my little room—so small the toilet was in the same area as my typewriter and the little television set I sometimes looked at.

I spotted a pencil and picked it up. I figured I'd start with something truly insignificant, like this old No. 2 yellow pencil with the eraser on the end.

"Okay, with this pencil I can write a grocery list or a love note or a song or a suicide note or the great American novel," I muttered to myself, not really feeling anything.

But as I played along, just going through the motions of looking for positive uses of this wooden pencil, I began to shift inside. I began to feel awe, surprise, and even wonder.

I then looked at the other end of the pencil.

"Wow! An eraser!" I exclaimed, but now I was sincere. I began to sense that this pencil was a genius invention. It's basically just a stick, but I could use it to write amazing things, and if I didn't like what I wrote, I could use the eraser to make it disappear. What magic!

After a few minutes of doing the pencil exercise, I felt different. I was lighter. Happier. I smiled

more. I looked around my little room and appreciated what was there. It was a turning point in my
life.

Today I sometimes get in my hot tub and look
at the stars and give thanks for my life, as I now live
the lifestyle of the rich and famous. Where I was
and where I am is so dramatically different that it
feels like the past was a past life.

And it all started with feeling grateful for right
now.

— Joe

Find *something* in your world that you love *now*—a pet,
a person, a pencil. Maybe just a sandwich.

Breathe slowly, and dwell on the entire space surrounding that object of love.

The smell of the pencil.

The texture of the lettuce in the sandwich.

The tone of voice of your grandparent.

This is sharpening your awareness of the complexity
of love in time and space. It captures more of your senses than you often realize. Sometimes you don't notice the
subtle signs of love from the future speaking to you in the
present. You have to remember how many ways love can
make itself known.

And then, remember the future. Don't wish. Don't
want. *Remember.* Remember the details. Was your soul
mate warm-blooded, or did he or she always turn up the
heat? Remember stupid, or seemingly stupid, things. Start
remembering your lover's smell. Remember the places you
frequented just prior to meeting him or her, and go there.
This will exponentially accelerate the connection to this

person. Even if it doesn't on a technical basis, starting to frequent a different place will open you to new experiences. You cannot lose.

Q: How can you remember a better life for yourself when the present moment feels full of lack, limitation, and sorrow?

First, nothing I'm speaking about is a replacement for treating serious mental-health issues. The Remembering Process is not a substitute for good therapy or other medical attention. If you are depressed or angry, I urge you to get help.

To use the technique, play, positivity, and possibility have to be like second nature. It's impossible to do it without access to them. Joe is one of many teachers who help people clear their blocks to those states.

My grandfather was a dancer, acclaimed gardener, factory worker, father, immigrant, and celebrator of the wonderful, small joys in life. He was also the only survivor in a family of 13. Nazis exterminated his parents and brothers and sisters, and they were never seen again after his late teens. Then he spent the rest of World War II in a Russian labor camp. If all you've had sucks, I would challenge you to find something worse than living through genocide. Grandpa was a hero and teacher to me. We enjoyed food, movies, sightseeing, and just the simple joy of being together. I know the thick, limiting feeling of sorrow, but I've had the privilege of seeing how much control we have over our perspective.

This moment is full of possibility.

While your brain chemistry can keep you from that joy, and as uncomfortable as it can be otherwise, it's not true unless you decide it is.

There are different brain states. A defensive brain state puts you into a reptilian stance on life, whereas the part of the brain that uses the Remembering Process on a practical or metaphysical level is your more advanced, evolved human brain. If you are in emotional pain, real or perceived, you won't have access to the process. So, first things first.

Also, it's essential to take care of your time machine, your physical body. Lots of water, rest, and healthy foods allow you to function highly and nimbly. When you're firing on all cylinders, you can pick up on subtle cues from the universe, and start to remember your future past. That being said, a technique is great when, even before it's working fully, it calls you to live your best life and be your best self. Let's say you believe that "life sucks" but want to try the technique anyway. Start with "remembering" how much life sucked before it got great. Agree with what is, and remember it as the stepping-stone to so much wisdom. Remember how you dissected each thing that sucks and painted pictures about what a positive change would look like in that area. Remember how this darkness taught you things that you were able to share with others. Now take it a step further . . .

Remember how the parents of missing children created more love and compassion in the world by establishing laws and resources for families of other missing children.

Remember how people who are terminally ill say and do the things that they've known they wanted to.

Remember how much you appreciated the success and happiness that came because you understood how deeply it contrasted with the old feelings.

Remember how you started piecing together happiness by counting tiny blessings.

Remember how you reached out and got help in many ways.

Remember that this moment was a point in time before your situation changed for the better and that you never looked back.

This is a great mental tool to help carry you forth.

Q: If you are diagnosed with cancer or another serious illness, can you remember past it?

Mari Kurko, founder of the holistic-health resource MamaShine Wellness, once responded to this by saying, "There is the mind and the body component to healing. Remembering our attitudes is a precursor to remembering the physical changes."

The Remembering Process has had incredible and miraculous effects. Still, I haven't seen incidents where people can cut themselves and "remember" it healing in real time in front of their eyes, for instance. I do know of individuals who, after receiving a diagnosis, "remembered" their most positive, inspired attitudes; and this has helped lead to their healing.

Having the grace to accept, assess, and make good decisions is something in the realm of great thinking. "Remembering" we were meditative and had epiphanies that created healing in our minds and hearts and families is very reachable.

In the event that an illness is curable, remembering your life *after* the illness is wonderful. Remember the first meal after treatment. Remember your lifestyle choices based upon lessons learned.

Remembering makes discipline so much easier. The brain is much more apt to run when it can *remember* having run.

The Remembering Process is one tool in a host of life's realities, circumstances, and previous choices, although the mystery of which illnesses are too much for our earthly bodies to fight is way bigger than any one methodology or mind. There is a certain point at which the mystery is too great for any one method, writer, or person.

When it's our time to go, it seems to be just that. Still, remembering how positive we became no matter what was going on is a huge step forward in life.

Q: Can the Remembering Process help when I'm feeling despair?

In a song from my forthcoming album, I sing the lyric, "Agree to the world inside."

When we feel despair, the Remembering Process is a wonderful tool for this because it is so simple. As gentle guidance, it encourages us to accept this moment as an absolutely essential link in the chain of our recovery from distress.

We can remember how free we felt after this trial and that this very moment was part of the turning tide. Sometimes that tide dissipates rapidly; sometimes it's more of a process. Still, seeing this moment exactly as it is and as being essential to the healing process loosens our ego's grip and relieves suffering.

> *Do you remember freedom from whatever you thought was hurting you and how that helped you shift? I seem to remember that.*

To use the process means that you feel on a deep level that you create your life and your reality. When you're suffering, this is hard to do. I don't know if it's 100 percent true that I create every aspect of my reality, to be honest. I know that I create a very high percentage. I round up to 100 percent as a gift to myself. That stance has created more possibility and has proven itself to be the most empowering idea I've known in this lifetime. I'll let someone else deal with the exact figures. I try each day to live from the assertion that I am 100 percent responsible for whatever is in front of me. When someone cuts me off in traffic, though, I do sometimes forget it. It's human.

But this I know: I rarely, if ever, benefit from living as a victim, regardless of how recklessly someone has turned into my lane.

The same applies to the Remembering Process, too. I have no idea the exact amount that it influences my life. I have no tools or rulers to measure its influence other than waking up each day living my dreams. I remembered the finish lines of marathons, the creation of a studio for recording music, and the opportunity to release a book. All of these have come true.

So I urge you to suspend the brain a bit and just feel how relieved you were when an elegant solution created movement where there was stagnation. Feel the intense joy that the witch was dead and the sun rose.

If even a brief moment of hope is what you get, consider that movement. Keep practicing like this and see what unfolds. Instead of pushing against the problem, relax and remember the lightness. Is there an ounce of relief? That's a start.

Q: What if what you remember is wrong? In other words, what if you remember things and later find out that what you remembered was totally off base?

Course correction exists at all times in life. Sometimes it takes a major wrong turn to understand where we want to go. Contrast is a primary tool that our higher self uses to teach us and show us the path. "The path" is not a perfect one. It just involves simple questions like, "Is this in the flow?" or "Is this congruent with my purpose?" Sometimes the best tool for answering that question is some good old-fashioned discomfort. Our backs teach us how to lift correctly in the same exact way.

"Man is made God's plaything, and that is the best part of him. Therefore every man and woman should live life accordingly, and play the noblest games. . . . What, then, is the right way of living? Life must be lived as play."

— Plato, *Laws*

If the path is not a perfect one, neither is the Remembering Process. It is not a catchall, remote control for life and reality. It's a tool, a guidance system, an accelerator. Mixed with discernment and hard work, it's a potent and exciting ally.

There is an assumption that the person using the process has a general sense of discernment. If not, that has to be developed first. It should be fairly obvious if one feels clearer, happier, and more connected to his or her ideal situation. There is playfulness to children in a sandbox. Sometimes they have to build a few sand castles before they reach their ideal palace. The Remembering Process doesn't take the place of trial and error. It does, however, give us major advantages as those trials and errors take their inevitable place. It gives us confidence that the mistakes are just course-correcting feedback en route to that which we want.

Q: How do you know that the Remembering Process isn't just "magical thinking" or a delusion?

None of us knows the exact nature of what is going on in this world. There is a great mystery that we are all throwing ourselves open to every day, or closing to every day. Sometimes we have different forms, mind-sets, and tools required all within the same hour, just to navigate this life. I've had profound experiences of magic, influence, and synchronicity. I've probably had profound instances of delusion, too. But in the end, I agree with this lyric from "Thinking Amelia," sung by singer/songwriter Deb Talan: "Expecting to fly doesn't sound so bad to me."

Certainly there will be critics of any technique. There are always detractors in the great game of life, no matter how you play it. There's no "thought" police. It's about what works. Keep in mind that different people have different ways of conceptualizing the world. My best advice is less criticism and more of the wisdom found in the adage "Live and let live."

Simply put, the Remembering Process works. It has brought outrageous joy to my life in the form of problem solving, possibility, creativity, and expression, to name just a few. As we've shown, it has accelerated the musical growth of my good friend, Joe. It has touched the lives of many. Try it! If it doesn't work for you, ignore it. If it does, welcome to the rest of your life. Or the beginning . . . or both.

I firmly believe it has influenced my life in both outcome and outlook for the better, consistently, for many years. It's one tool in a complex box of life's tools. It's not a device I employ to ignore my body and its needs for safety and balance. Used in tandem with a grounded approach, it's absolute joy unleashed on Earth!

Q: At what point does feeling come into play in remembering? It seems very heady—all thinking, no feeling.

So what does the Remembering Process feel like?

Like a gentle "streeeeeeeetch" and "ahhhh"! It feels like a sweet, foggy memory or a vivid "Heck, yeah!" The whole process is about feeling the joy of what you wanted in its completion. Your future self is sending a wave of happiness upon the completion of whatever you thought you wanted.

It's done. It's here. Your future self is planning the party, basking in the glow and waiting for you to catch up. It's your destiny fulfilled, and you're already feeling the fulfillment while your physical reality catches up. It's the calm of knowing. It's the confidence of major wins under your belt.

The process makes me want to jump and shout and smile from ear to ear. I feel the pride of tapping into my deepest resources and highest self, meditating on the vastness of my soul. It can give you the tingle of anticipation because you just know it's about to get good. Really good.

It's all of this and more. Using this process removes the vice of fear and tension that is based on thinking within a reality where dreams don't happen. Instead, your heart is open and your muscles relaxed as you walk calmly to your best life.

You release old thoughts and the need for control that comes when you take ownership of your reality. Instead of the push and pull of wanting, the Remembering Process has an overarching feeling of ease, play, and wonder. There is an airy feeling in my heart and mind as I play with the process. I float into play. Then I hit a more potent memory, and I get a rush of positive energy. A little heat in the face, and champagne feelings that follow.

It's hard not to smile and light up when you think of all that your future self has accomplished. It's also hard not to feel humbled and grateful when you think of all the people you've helped by tapping into your future self. Did you help homeless people in your community? Maybe you put a family member through school. Did you "remember" a song for your fiancée that made your wedding a day she'll never forget?

Don't mistake the gentle breeze of inspiration for a lack of feeling. What we've done is take some of the heavier feelings out of the equation—fear that can take us down and false pride that can stifle. There is a gentle feeling of nostalgia that will bring you to your desired place in the family of things. One of the surprises is that you will find your life closer to your dreams than you ever previously believed you'd be, and it will be gentle and quick to get there. Once you play with the throttle of time, you can really get places quickly. So, yes, there is subtlety to the feeling states. They are powerful nonetheless.

You have to slow your mind as your reality accelerates. You must use all of your senses to align with your future self. Remember the tactile subtleties of the cotton shirts your future self favored. Remember the smell of the cedars as your future self made that extra trip to the woods you craved, and the smell of new books as you put yourself through that degree program with ease and joy. Remember the healthful foods you cooked sizzling in the pan as you ate better for your desired body. Remember that you quit smoking and how all manner of smells opened back up to you. The technique is very sensual in nature. You will have to relax and seek clues from all angles.

What many people consider to be deep desire for an outcome is actually a profound fear that it won't happen, and that fear comes with a great deal of inner sensation; when you remember, it kind of floats sweetly through your being.

Are you willing to give up the roller coaster of angst and release for a sweet relief of knowing? Will you lose your edge, or will you gain a deeper understanding of how things can get done easier and more joyfully?

The feeling is that of a positive and fluid improvisation with life. You are agreeing with the current moment because you know it was an essential piece of history in the direction of the reality you remember.

This is definitely not for everyone. I know many people who prefer to suffer for their achievements. Not all of them know they have this desire, but their external states reflect their internal inclination. I made a decision that I wanted to enjoy life, enjoy work, and not struggle any harder than I had to. I still work more often than most people I know, but it's doing the work I love and dreamed I'd do. To me, it feels more like relaxing into a deep stretch than forcing or pushing my way through life.

Q: How can the Remembering Process help me get stuff done?

Productivity is an area that I've had plenty of personal experience and strain in. I've often found myself feeling intimidated by tasks and deadlines. And it's no wonder given the nature and origin of the word *deadline,* as explained on the website Words@Random:

> The word *deadline* first appeared as an American coinage that referred to the line around a military prison beyond which soldiers were authorized to shoot escaping prisoners. According to Lossing's *History of the Civil War* (1868), "Seventeen feet from the inner stockade was the 'dead-line,' over which no man could pass and live." This use is also found in Congressional records as early as 1864: "The 'dead line,' beyond which the prisoners are not allowed to pass." The citations for this use dry up at the end of the 19th century.

Most difficulties with productivity come from a misconception, fear, and tightness about time that can be traced all the way back to a fear of death.

The task at hand may be a reasonable one, but the fears associated with doing or not doing that task become a catalyst for a fight-or-flight response, leading to a shallow, dualistic concept of time and space.

I remember that I wrote future books in a cabin. I remember plugging in the Universal Audio preamp, an aptly named piece of equipment in my studio that I use when I want to record my thoughts before I write them down. I remember that over the last two days, I wrote 14 hours straight each day. I love pressure, and I love deadlines.

I remember that the book was excellent. I remember that money flowed in and never stopped. I remember that I was below 180 pounds and built.

I remember that the book was a fluid and wonderful experience. It is right now.

This book is complete and finished before I write it. In some reality, you are reading it already. If I fear not finishing, I put a break or disconnect in the time and space continuum. The Remembering Process helps me erase that fear and frees me up to become more productive, because I already know the book will be finished.

While writing my portion of the book, I'd often find solitude and increased productivity in my studio. After writing late into the night one evening, I got under the covers in my studio's guest bedroom and eagerly cracked open the book I'd just bought: *Personal Development for Smart People,* written by the esteemed personal-development expert Steve Pavlina. Living in unified time, and in a world of resonance, synchronicity, and unity, I was delighted to find the following exercise that essentially articulates and illustrates another beautiful way to enter the realm of remembering, and the peace and possibility that accompanies. Here's Steve's exercise to help you enter the remembering realm:

The Time-Travel Meditation

This is one of my favorite meditation exercises, and I think you'll really enjoy it, too. First go to a place where you can physically relax. Lie down or sit comfortably, close your eyes, and breathe deeply for a few minutes. Imagine a special room in your mind's eye, one with two comfortable chairs facing each other. You're sitting in one chair, and in the other chair is your future self—the person you'll become five years from now. Your future self knows everything you know, as well as everything that will happen to you during the next five years. Now imagine having a conversation with this person. Ask anything you want, and listen for the answers.

When you're ready, ask your future self to get up and leave the room, and imagine that your past self from five years ago walks in and sits down. You are *this* person's future self. Take a moment to recall what your past self has been going through. What was your life like exactly five years ago? Imagine your past self asking you questions about how your life turned out; and see yourself answering with empathy, understanding, and reassurance. Tell your past self about some of the challenges that will be coming up in the years ahead, challenges that you've already faced.

When you're finished connecting with your past self, imagine that your future self reenters the room and all three of you stand up. Your bodies begin to glow and become translucent. You float toward each other and merge into a single being of light. When this happens, you may experience an intense release of emotion. The three of you are now an integrated whole, a single being who exists outside of time. This being is the real you.

I encourage you to try this meditation at least once, even if you've never meditated before. It will help you recognize that there's a timeless nature to your existence, that you're more than just a physical being moving forward through time. In the presence of this awareness, your momentary worries will shrink, replaced by feelings of expansiveness and connectedness.

From *Personal Development for Smart People,* by Steve Pavlina. Reprinted with permission.

Q: I know what I want to achieve in my life with the Remembering Process. Where do I go from here? What else can I do to increase my chances of success?

As I mentioned earlier, when you "need" or want with tension, you push your object of desire further from your present field because those emotions connote lack. Here you can use gratitude as the gateway to the expanded consciousness, and you get to gratitude with the Remembering Process.

Remember how clear your next e-mail was. Remember how great your next meal was. Changing one word—"I *want*" to "I *remember*"—jogs a different part of your brain, one that can cause a breakthrough, like your own "Bannister Effect." If you recall, Roger Bannister was the first person to run a sub-4-minute mile, although once he broke that barrier, other runners began to do it routinely. What this showed was that many other runners were capable of running this fast, but first, someone had to show them it was possible. This phenomenon was subsequently dubbed "The Bannister Effect." Runners could now break the 4-minute barrier because they could remember that it had been successfully done before; it was no longer an imagined impossibility.

Remembering that *we have already* begins the transition to unified consciousness. It creates a relaxed sense of abundance that stimulates our higher self. The leap is to *now* be grateful for all that we are and all that we have in planes of consciousness that we cannot yet see in this earthly walk. Otherwise, it's like holding a seed to an oak tree and being upset about not possessing a tree.

We hold the seeds to all that we desire in our imagination. We just have to acknowledge that the full tree of pure potential within our lives exists in these seeds.

John Coltrane, an American jazz saxophonist and composer, said, "I start in the middle of a sentence and move both directions at once." Our past and present are accessible in both directions from this very point. This is how time works. However, it comes with a caveat: The Remembering Process doesn't substitute for methodical work, which has its own unique place in getting things done.

It also doesn't take the place of being a professional in your craft. This is best expressed in a quote by writer David Milch, the creator of the HBO TV show *Deadwood,* when he said that "visions come to prepared spirits." So, while he is "remembering" and dreaming up characters, stories, and scenes, he has the background and skill set to work with it.

Just like gravity works on everyone, some of us train our bodies to move through that reality of gravity with more grace than others. The same applies to the Remembering Process and quantum time. If we train ourselves in a creative field, there is a readiness to perceive, receive, and express that which is being shared with us from the place where time is elastic.

The more you practice the Remembering Process, the more it will become a reliable tool that will feel right to try in any number of situations—whether you're attempting to overcome a fear or become more creative, productive, calm, loving, or healthful. If you use it with others, it can even help you strengthen your relationships as you build the bond of shared dreams and shared play. However, can there ever be too much of a good thing? Next we'll discuss when to pull back from using the process.

STRIKING THE RIGHT BALANCE

"Time is but the stream I go a-fishing in."
— Henry David Thoreau

The Remembering Process is not an attempt to get around the normal, physical world. As long as we are in this human body, we need to enjoy and respect that reality.

Even though I believe that the Remembering Process is effective and can speed up your path to your goals, it's not a substitute for hard work, healthy habits, and practice. You can't take a spiritual bypass to your problems.

Spiritual bypassing is when people try to live in the spiritual world all the time, relying on just thinking or praying or remembering to solve all their problems for them effortlessly. It's like a person who goes to church and prays to God to find a job, and then just sits at home and waits for God to answer the prayer. It doesn't work that way . . .

there is no spiritual slam dunk that delivers without any effort on your part. You have to put yourself in the right place to receive what God or the Universe will give to you.

In other words, simply remembering that you sold a screenplay for $1 million doesn't make it happen. It helps you to envision it, move confidently toward your dream, and take the steps necessary to get to that point. However, you still have to write a darn good script and submit it to the right people at the right time.

You'll know you're in danger of spiritual bypassing when your basic affairs are not in order: if your bills aren't paid, you're not taking care of your health, your house is a mess, you've ignored the jury-duty summons that arrived in the mail last month, and your lawn isn't watered. Another sure sign is that you're not keeping up with your relationships with other people or ignoring your friends' concerns.

If someone interviews the five people closest to you without your being present, and asks if you're emotionally available, they should all answer yes. You should be fully present for your loved ones; if they feel like you're not grounded or have stopped caring, then you have a problem. It can be easy to get lost in the spiritual realm when you're trying to improve yourself, but you have to keep one foot planted in the Newtonian "now." Life works better in balance.

You'll know you're in balance if you feel an overall sense that you're connected to what matters and spending your days living your best life. You're not on the right path if people who barely know you think you're a spiritual guru, but at the same time you're neglecting your kids at home.

So absolutely work the Remembering Process, but don't lose track of the tangible realities that will move you toward your goals. The process is "part of a complete breakfast," not the whole breakfast. At best it appears we are only meant to enjoy unified time *some* of the time while we are here, with a few exceptions. There are people who enter enlightened states in this life and are imperturbable. For the rest of us, mortal life is a given, and we travel in varying degrees of speed and access toward the unknown. And strewn along our path are choices. How shall we make them?

Fate vs. Free Will

The Remembering Process allows you to bypass the "fate vs. free will" continuum and start a creation process that is vaster than anything on the duality plane.

Occasionally, I'm asked something along the lines of, "What is the relationship between 'letting go and letting God,' and using your conscious will to remember the truth of who you are?" In other words, where is that fine line between "controlling" the Universe by forcing your own will versus allowing the Universe to do its thing and staying open to receiving?

Do we step back and surrender completely, allowing our spirit to be in charge of our reality by staying in the moment and not thinking of the future at all? Or do we step forward and take risks as co-creators with our spirit by doing the Remembering Process? If we do step forward, is there a point we should let go? And if so, where exactly is that point? For most people "on the path," it seems that the co-creative choice feels more exciting, truthful, and even logical, yet often at the same time they may experience an internal conflict about this on a subconscious, or cellular, level.

My own bias is that the great creative powers within us are a teaching mechanism from the Creator's energy, independent of any particular archetype or religious notion of that Creator. We are all a creation story of biblical proportions.

When we remember, we resonate sympathetically with the infinite. Our earthly desires are a great trail marker to get back into our higher selves. This means that our desires get our attention. They call us forward from where we are to where we want to be. If we want to move to a new town, it's because there is a better life calling us. Maybe it's more comfort. More family time. Regardless of the "what," there is a better life calling to each of us, and our desires are the carrots that get us moving. At the end of that trail is our creative fulfillment.

Metaphysical painter Alex Grey (www.alexgrey.com) says, "Artists are called to fulfill their creative potential. They elect this path for themselves or feel fated to it." If we broaden this perspective with the notion that all humans are in effect "creating their lives," we can assert that our desires are the call to fulfill our creative human potential. With the Remembering Process, we are creating a relationship and harmony between our animal selves and our higher creator selves. One is completely focused on survival, while the other is infinite and has no birth or death.

At its core, we are tapping into another dimension. It could be another dimension of our brain, or another dimension of reality. I believe it's the place where those two entities interface.

Because the brain is our time-travel device, our animal instincts are here to ground us but can also hold us back. Fear, adrenaline, cortisol, and any other stress responses keep us right here in our present reality. I can understand that if the body thinks it's about to fight, it needs all of its resources right here and now. No time travel. This traveling and crossing realms works great for ideas and planning, but not as much for washing dishes, running marathons, or throwing punches. An integrated dance between the physical and the metaphysical allows one to act on all of the inspiration that becomes available in time-travel mode. That's why you can "remember" a life filled with peace and simplicity, but *you still have to wash your dishes.*

This tension creates the music of life, like the tension on a guitar string creates a sonic possibility. When we tune in correctly, we can create a harmony. Too much tension toward the animal side, we snap the string. Too loose and overly focused on the infinite side, we are floppy and unusable by the universal symphony.

Striking this balance is the goal.

The sweet spot is to breathe life into the middle place such that both extremes melt. By being clear about our desires and grateful for their existence, we strike that balance. Recall that "wanting" these things pushes them away, while being grateful for them now says *yes* to the Universe. Possibility is spoken here.

Keys to the Remembering Process are self-love, self-esteem, and self-awareness. Don't wait until you find out how wildly abundant you actually, truly are now to begin treating yourself that way. If you found out friends of yours were rich and successful, and started treating them better after you realized this, they might not trust your intentions.

All that you seek is already in your field. Be impressed and grateful for yourself at *this* moment.

Stay Open to the Lessons on the Path

In essence, all you need is the feeling and a scant few details of your imagined or "remembered" future to bring it into reality. All the while, you will be confronted with any tensions or lessons you are supposed to learn in the current dimension. You cannot bypass this learning part of the process.

Eva Pierrakos, in the following passage from her book, *The Pathwork of Self-Transformation,* explains why humans experience as much tension as they do:

> Time is a very limiting existential modality. It is a fragment, cut from a wider and freer dimension of experience. The vague knowledge that the time at your disposal is limited in this earth-dimension creates a special tension. You, therefore, strive to get out of this limitation of "time," straining as a dog pulls at its leash.

As she explains, we want to look forward to our future, but the march of time also means decay and death—so we may also dig in our heels and fear moving forward in our development. Maturing means aging, and aging means dying. No wonder some of us get stunted in our personal growth and obsess about erasing any evidence of aging. There are literally thousands of wrinkle creams on the market, but there's not one cream that can help you come to peace with the creator within you.

And that's what you are: a creator. You are the only person who can live your life. You get to wake up every morning and create the life you choose, molding it this way and that until you're not just satisfied, but jubilant about it.

Of course, it's not always a smooth journey, nor should it be. How boring would it be if you were never challenged in any way? Each time you use the Remembering Process, you will encounter specific issues to resolve. Simply welcome them. It's an inherent part of the path of transformation, which, if you're reading this book and you're human, you are clearly traveling.

When it came time for me to go into the Rubicon recording studio and sing, play guitar, and record my own songs, I was nervous. I was excited, too. But I knew I was about to record with some legends in music, such as the other Joe Vitale who had recorded with Neil Young. And now he was going to record with first-timer *me*.

I expressed my concerns to Daniel. We instantly went to the future and started speaking as if the recording were over.

"I remember that the sessions went so smoothly that we were surprised," Daniel said. "Your playing and singing were in perfect harmony. The group came together as if we had played those songs for years. I think I remember that we did all the recording in one day, not the scheduled two."

I picked up on what Daniel was doing and joined in.

"I remember that we did so great in recording the songs for *Strut!* that we couldn't stop smiling," I added. "I felt comfortable and really loved the process."

We spent a few minutes like that, talking about the recording session in the past tense, upping the energy, sending out a signal that the future had to feel.

When I picked up the other Joe Vitale at the airport, I immediately loved the guy. We had so much in common that it was unreal. I also took the time to ask him for advice. I told him I was nervously excited. He said, "That's great! You don't want to go in there feeling nothing. Nervousness means you care."

I asked for advice on how to sing my songs. He said, "I just met you. I don't know your songs, and I haven't heard you sing. But you are doing this for a reason. I say go into the studio and testify!"

His words excited me. Between the remembering Daniel and I had done and my conversation with the other Joe Vitale, I went into the studio and hit a home run. The songs went easily and effortlessly. Even when I belted out a 13-second primal screaming of the word *strut,* my voice held strong. Everyone was moved.

We ended up recording for two days rather than the one we "remembered," but that didn't matter at all. All of our remembering elevated our energy and our confidence, and the end result is an album we all absolutely love.

— Joe

Here's my own example of staying open to the lessons on the path: When I built a walkway at my home, I hired contractors to help me with the project. Almost immediately I was confronted with my overly generous notion of trust.

One contractor, whom I paid in advance of starting work, stopped halfway through the job, giving me stories of sick children and hospital visits (he had actually been in jail). He took the money, quit working, and became un-reachable. Although I could have viewed the incident as strictly a miserable experience, I found that it gave me the opportunity to work on boundaries, trust, obstacles, and anger—intrinsic lessons I needed from the project.

How do I know I needed it? If I didn't, I would have picked a better contractor and paid in installments, as is common with reputable workers in that field.

Accepting and not resisting these opportunities allowed me to finish the project and learn the appropriate lessons. I have since chosen with a wiser heart and mind and had great success in projects. The key is that I was able to sketch my initial feeling and ideas and let the project arrive more fully here.

At my studio, this is how we make albums, too. People would be amazed by how vague the memories of the albums are before they arrive in their fully embodied self. We often have to go through lots of clearing along the way.

A Question of Morals

"There is nothing wrong in wanting to get rich. The desire for riches is really the desire for a richer, fuller, and more abundant life; and that desire is praise worthy."

—Wallace D. Wattles

We use the Remembering Process to develop our true nature, the heart of our best life and true manifestation. Is it shallow to use unified consciousness to create wealth, toys, and worldly success, especially when others in the world are suffering?

This is a duality thought—a judgment. You can be wealthy *and* be deep, spiritual, giving, and generous. You can also be poor and shallow. They are not mutually exclusive qualities. You don't need to give away all your earthly possessions and live in a hut in the wilderness to be spiritually whole.

In the Tao Te Ching, Lao-tzu says that the master observes the world but trusts his inner vision. He allows things to come and go, and his heart is open as the sky. He doesn't mention that it's harder to do that when you are hungry, angry, lonely, or tired. Some people who read this will be in far more difficult circumstances than my own or many others'. Maybe you are reading this in the midst of a firefight in Afghanistan or in a poor neighborhood in India.

Where do we find the strength, courage, and wisdom to live fully and powerfully no matter what? It is especially in these challenging environments that a new interpretation, a new way of seeing, can support us in the world.

When you realize there is nothing lacking, the whole world belongs to you.

Taking care of yourself the best you can, honoring your desires and your visions, and seeking your best self-expression is all you are called to do. There is a certain air of confidence you give off when you are content to be yourself, without trying to measure up to anyone else. You don't need to be the most beautiful, the richest, or the most talented to give off this air of confidence; "average" people who are content with themselves are magnetic.

Give yourself permission to relax into your wonderful, authentic self.

Some people do not achieve a greater level of oneness, success, and flow because they are stuck in the mode of trying to please others. And of course it doesn't work. What works is being comfortable with yourself; then you will effortlessly attract people to you.

My meetings with Daniel are upbeat and unpredictable. We call our free-form conversation "popcorning" as we never know where it will pop and we don't edit each other. We talk about whatever surfaces, whether or not it's related to music. Whenever there is a snag or an uncertainty about something related to the goal of making great albums, we fall back to remembering.

As I was writing songs for what was to become my first singer-songwriter album, I wondered what the songs were. I "remembered" that there were 12 songs. How did I remember that? I simply used my mind to see the cover of the CD. Obviously at that point with Daniel, the cover didn't exist. It was a potential. A possibility.

However, at the same time, the CD existed *in the future*, on some sort of time line yet to be manifest. When I looked to see it in the future, as a finished result, the image was hazy, but it let me know that it was real. It didn't matter if the CD as I remembered it matched the CD I actually created. The idea was to get the creative juices flowing.

The completed album *Strut!* ended up with 11 tracks instead of 12. Did that mean that my remembering was done wrong? Not at all. I learned that when you remember something, it's like remembering what I ate yesterday: I know I ate, and I have a good idea of what it was, but I may not remember *exactly*.

Still, the remembering helped me in the creating.

— Joe

The world is a total reflection of our inner state. Are there other ways of looking at that? Sure. Are they as empowering? Absolutely not.

In a world as relative as the one we are speaking of, we have the responsibility to scan and hold fast to the most empowering version of the truth that we can discern at any given moment. Not the most "altruistic," though perhaps it would be. Not the "easiest," but perhaps it would be.

It comes down to an inner vision and intuition and guidance system that becomes adept at observing for true growth and empowerment. Not the scratching of itchy desires, but the vibration of genuine soul dharma, our most authentic life's work.

We are called to see the world as ourselves—to see that we are all connected and responsible for one another. Once inside a unified field of possibility, greed and altruism become unified, and helping ourselves allows us to reach out to others.

For example, Bono, of the renowned rock band U2, lives the life of a worldly rock star while offering a hand to many in need. Oprah builds an empire and empowers millions in the process. Joe creates his dreams while writing and teaching others how to create theirs.

My own studio and artist-development program at Rubicon allows me to do what I love—recording albums—and at the same time, I help others live the musical life they dream of. You can do the same, and it's very satisfying. Remember a life that includes service both to yourself and others.

I remember sitting on my office deck, among the trees and birds and squirrels, reflecting on a song I'd written in the future but not yet in the moment. My mind whirled around the idea of "Be kind" as a mantra or theme. Then I started to receive lines. The result was the standout song on my album *Strut!* titled "Everybody's Goin' thru Something."

Did I write the song or remember the song? Both. In the future it already existed. As I remembered it, I wrote it. The future Joe and the present Joe are one anyway. The convergence let me be a secretary for the future's prose.

Don't hurt your head thinking about this. In the future, you already get it.

For now, remember what you got.

— Joe

In order to be successful, one must create value for others.

Jack Canfield, known for his Chicken Soup for the Soul series, uses the term *loverage* to convey this idea. It's a two-step method that requires you to connect with the heart of your desires and dreams first. Then you determine how to create the maximum value for others via that dream. As an example, my two work loves are recording albums and personal growth and development. To be successful, I just need to continue to do what I love while refining how effective and helpful I can be to others.

Study and trust your desires. Get clear about who *you* are and what *you* want. Strike the right balance between the Newtonian now and your spiritual endeavors. Dream big, but do the work that's involved. This will start calling your best life and destiny to you.

And as you work toward your goals and use the Re-membering Process as a helpful supplement, trust that you're already where you're meant to be and that every-thing will happen at just the right time.

HOW FAR CAN WE GO?

"It's entirely up to you how you use your imagination. . . . You make the decision, and are therefore responsible for its effect on the world."

— Neville Goddard

When we expect that all we dream of is not only possible but has also happened already, it creates a certain amount of confidence. Confidence and self-esteem *must* be cultivated in various ways in the Newtonian, old-brain way. A basic belief in our worth is part of the relaxed and unified field needed to make the leaps we are speaking of.

Having an expectation that your best life is out there somewhere in the time and space continuum is a wonderful way to live. The Remembering Process lets you call it in gently toward this plane so that you can enjoy and share it. Even if this weren't so, your life would still be better.

It's like saying, "If I don't become an international rock star or a star quarterback, the pursuit and full effort toward that potential is actually the grand prize." The process of living toward your best life *is* your best life.

Even if the unified-state step of the technique doesn't totally resonate with you, you are still likely to have a great life after ten years of focusing and creating it. It's a winning proposition all around. I've seen the Remembering Process accelerate my own and other peoples' progress in ways that are thrilling and belief shattering.

Mayo, an 18-year-old rapper, is one of my music mentoring clients. He has already put the Remembering Process into action, and here's how he describes it:

I remember my first DWI. I remember the first time I cheated on my girlfriend. I remember dreaming of being an NBA superstar. Those moments and thoughts are in the past, and the past isn't going to change.

Change begins with remembering your future.

I remember driving with Dan in his freshly cleaned Lexus, listening to my first album. The ice cream that we bought at Sandy's tasted sweeter than ever. We didn't say one word about the album because we didn't have to; we knew what we had accomplished.

I remember spending nights in my room writing rhymes while my peers downed beer. I remember focusing on my family and art, and not letting distractions keep me anchored. These are the things I remember in order to live up to my full potential.

The mind is powerful, and when you use it right you can accomplish anything in the world. When you store positive thoughts in your head, the little voice that tells you that "you can't do this" goes away. Every time I'm faced with a dilemma, I remember how I overcame that particular obstacle. Then I put it into action.

There are thousands of kids in the world right now filling out their first job application or writing their first song; the majority of those kids doubt their ability to get hired, and doubt that anyone will appreciate their music. Instead of doubting myself, I choose to remember what I'm capable of and put it into use.

Trust yourself and keep your word; nothing's going to hold you back if you apply those two things into your everyday life.

The Remembering Process isn't one big daydream; it's a tool that allows you to break free from distractions and focus on your mission. *I remember performing onstage, looking out into the crowd and seeing hundreds of hands in the air, moving up and down like a seesaw.* Was I nervous? Intimidated? Hell, yeah. I remember it, though, and it's going to happen.

Reproduced by permission of Christian Mayo.

The Remembering Process gives you all that you seek—love, connection, health, wealth, peace . . . whatever you desire. If you have all of that somewhere in the time and space continuum and feel a connection to it, what would your life be like?

I don't mean that rhetorically; I mean really take a few minutes to imagine it. All of your desires have come to fruition. How do you feel? What does your life look like? What are the things that pull you the most, that make you the happiest?

It's okay that this is imagination for now—after all, as Neville Goddard said, "Is there anything in this world that wasn't first imagined? Name one thing or point at one thing in this world for me that is now considered to be real that wasn't first imagined." Everything—every item in your home, every play you've seen, every song on the radio, every medicine, every technology—came forth from the fertile ground of someone's creative mind. Your mind has that same kind of potency. You can imagine something into reality. That is your power as a Divine creator. What will you use your power to create for yourself, for your loved ones, and for the world? There are no limits on you.

It's usually more exciting to do the Remembering Process with another person. I've often spent a minute explaining how it works—just go into the future, past your desired outcome, and playfully recall whatever you can about the experience. But I've also seen the power of doing this process entirely alone.

For example, after recording my first singer/songwriter album, I imagined performing the songs live. I quickly received invitations to perform. My staff and I kicked around the idea of doing a concert. And the other Joe Vitale openly said that he wanted to play drums whenever I performed live.

Whew.

One of the issues for me became my health. I had gained weight when I backed off from exercising due to a foot injury. I needed to heal my wound (heel spur and tear in a ligament) and lose weight. I wanted to look good onstage and be able to stand and dance and otherwise move around.

But I didn't know how to accomplish any of that. The foot injury alone had been with me for years. And I had tried a long list of treatments to heal it, but it was still there. Sometimes it hurt so bad I couldn't drive, let alone walk or run. What was I going to do?

I then "remembered" a solution. I sat down and imagined that I was in the future—where my injury was healed, my weight was stabilized, and I was performing as much as I wanted (to thunderous applause). In this future, the things I had been concerned about were a distant past. From this future place, I started to "remember" how I had cured my foot and achieved my weight-loss goal.

None of it was perfectly remembered. After all, it's a memory. But just knowing that, in the future, I had the issues resolved was comforting, encouraging and even energizing. I speculated that I ran into a healer or a new healing treatment. I wondered if I had found a fun, new way to exercise and a nutrition program I enjoyed. I wasn't sure about any of it. That didn't matter. My future was certain. Remembering it made it so.

How I'd get there would remain a mystery for a while, but it would unfold. I knew it because I had remembered it. Now get this . . .

I went to Hawaii in early 2012 for a meeting with the Transformational Leadership Council. Among the attendees was a Chinese healer, and I went to one of his healing treatments on the beach, skeptical but eager to try anything. He worked on for me for maybe 20 minutes, basically sending energy to my injury. At the end, he said, "I closed the wound." I didn't believe him. But over the next two days, I was able to walk with greater ease.

Then, back in Texas, a friend invited me to meet the entrepreneurs behind a new piece of fitness equipment called Nexersys. I went, loved the people, and loved the product. It combines a video game with maneuvers that require you to use most of your body to accomplish. I could do it even as my foot completed its healing journey. It also helped that such legends as Jackie Chan and wrestler The Undertaker were using the Nexersys. It didn't take long for me to agree to add one to my own personal gym. I'm such a fan of the Nexersys now that the *Austin American-Statesman* newspaper called me and quoted me saying, "This is the first time in my entire life where I actually look forward to exercising!"

And then I entered the Bill Phillips Transformation program, a 12-week fitness discipline for transforming your body and mind. I knew Bill Phillips from ten years ago, when he had his Body for Life challenge. I loved him and his work. I took to "Transformation" easily, and had intense fun morphing my body into a fit ideal for myself.

From my perspective today, I attracted these solutions to long-standing problems by the energy in "remembering." I had solved the problems in the future.

— Joe

If you allow yourself to believe that you can imagine things into reality, could it make a difference in the world? In your world? Would you *act* differently in the world?

When I graduated from college, my brother Jeffrey gave me a plaque that said, "What would you attempt if you knew you could not fail?" Let the Remembering Process give you that kind of fearlessness—the thought that all you have to do is redeem what's already yours at some point in the future.

Our ideas about what is possible have evolved every 50 years, going back as far as history can be recorded. Even 15 years ago, our concepts of cell phones, computers, and the Internet were just little buds or seeds. Nanotechnology and other advances continue to expand and bend our minds to what is possible.

The fact that few have been able to fully explain, demonstrate, or compellingly label unified time does not make it less real, although I have a hunch that those who do know and use unified time generally keep it as a personal experience.

To step outside unified consciousness and name it— to speak about it—is somewhat like "dancing about architecture," to quote the inimitable Declan Patrick Aloysius MacManus, who is affectionately known as the singer Elvis Costello. There's a beautiful futility to it; we can try to explain the experience, but it doesn't translate perfectly to words. That doesn't mean it's not real, though. Gravity wasn't less real or potent prior to Newton discovering it. It was always here. People just weren't talking about it yet.

"The straight lines of time are actually threads of a web extending to infinity," Deepak Chopra writes in *The Way of the Wizard*. There's a logical order to Newtonian time—"I'll be there in five minutes," means the same thing to everyone—but unified time includes those five minutes and many other threads of time, extending forward and backward at once.

By its nature, unified time just is. And you can access it via your own personal mental time machine, the Remembering Process. Just like no one has any more entitlement to spiritual enlightenment than anyone else, the Remembering Process doesn't discriminate, either: There is no one out there who can do it better than you can. Any time you want, you can hop into that DeLorean in your mind, rev it up to 88 miles per hour, and activate the flux capacitor. All it takes are two words: *I remember.*

> Recently I went to Ohio to visit my mother in the hospital. While I was there, my brother-in-law told me about a classic American muscle car for sale. I wasn't really interested, but I wanted to pacify him so we went to look at it. It was a 1972 bright red Corvette Stingray. Upon first sight, I fell in love. It's an award-winning car with chrome under the hood. I bought it, too. But that isn't the interesting part.
>
> The wife of the owner of the car knew me. We graduated from the same high school in 1972. It was 2011 as we stood on her lawn. I have little memory of high school and have none of her. Even looking at the high-school yearbook later and seeing her picture didn't trigger anything.
>
> Later, back home in Texas, thinking about the Remembering Process, I was guided to look at old pictures. I made some coffee, then went and followed my intuition. These photos were from 10 to

20 years ago. I could remember them. There was my first wife, who passed away in 2004. There were my kitties, and they had passed away. There were the book signings and the friends who were so close to me back then. Each picture brought back a feeling, a memory, a person, a place.

Where did they all go?

As I looked at the pictures, remembering them and those moments made them real again. They were real once. Now they were just a memory. But the memory doesn't make them any less real.

Then it occurred to me that is how the Remembering Process works.

We "remember" the future—which seems as foggy as the past—but remembering it doesn't mean it didn't happen or won't happen. It's just a screen shot in the mind. If the past is foggy, but I know it was real, can't the future be foggy and yet be real, too?

In other words, as I write these words for you, it is my present and your past. But I was inspired to write them for you because my future self had already penned the words. I "remembered" having written them, and that guided me in this moment to start writing.

And here we are. I'm writing. You're reading. And both of the acts live in the past and were predicted in the future and exist right now in the present.

Pretty cool, right?

— Joe

Be, Do, Have. Act As If. Fake It Till You Make It.

There are no guarantees in the remembering game, although I can bet that if you don't think it will work, if you don't think it will give you a glimpse in the direction of your best life, you will be correct. This is a place where belief is an invitation to step into a different viewpoint in your mind and soul. If you're looking for advanced exercises in the area of faith in the vastness of your soul's power and the possibility of multiple dimensions, try it! Just play with the Remembering Process.

Learn to rely on the unseen forces—those forces that affect your spiritual antenna and cause "weather patterns" of a sort. They make quantum thinking, feeling, and travel more available to your body, brain, and spirit.

The best way to learn a language is to dive in. In my band, porterdavis, we have a mantra: "The best way to do something is to do it." My personal mantra is, "The best way to get what you want is to know what you want."

I loved the Remembering Process from the moment I learned it from Daniel. It sure made creating music easier and more fun. But I also began to use it in other areas.

When I was hired to write a book called *Faith,* I had no idea where to begin. Facing a blank sheet of paper is always a challenge as well as an opportunity. What was I going to write? I didn't know. I could just start typing, as the process of writing anything will lead to something.

But I wanted this to be easier, so I turned to remembering. I knew the book already existed in the future. How did I know that? I knew I would write it *somehow.* So of course it had to exist. What I had to do was remember it.

By just allowing my mind to wonder about the book, I began to get a sense of what was in it. I would—in my mind's eye—open the book and look at the Table of Contents. This let me peek into my own mind. While I didn't see everything clearly at first glance, I saw enough to make me confident.

At that point, I started writing. Once again, I was creating by remembering.

— Joe

I'm holding a book in my lap with a cover that says, "The Remembering Process." Did I tape that to an existing book? Maybe.

Is it spurring me forth? Yes.

The early phases of the Remembering Process might even be more important than the high-flying, time-defying, unified processes because they dislodge our animal fears and get us looser and moving in the direction of our dreams. They also help us clarify exactly what we want to "remember" and create our soul path.

Anything that doesn't make our lives better or empower us in a true sense should not be espoused as wisdom. *But,* we don't have to understand the molecular structure of cough syrup to enjoy a better night's sleep from it. All we need to do is adopt enough of these principles to gradually make our reality more joyful and fulfilled.

Goethe said, "Man is not born to solve the problems of the universe, but to find out where the problems begin, and then to take his stand within the limits of the intelligible." Do it. Take your stand. As you play with the Remembering

Process, over time you will discover a clear distinction—that it's not so much the Law of Attraction at work here as it is the Law of Allowing. You have a right to your destiny, your abundance, and with this technique you *allow* it instead of supposing it might not have happened. Bear in mind that even in resistance there is beauty, and that tension allows for growth, emptiness, and fullness. Accept that your resistance and your skepticism exist, and then give yourself permission to let them go—maybe just this once. Allow yourself to tap into your birthright by becoming who you are meant to be.

Somehow, at its highest, the Remembering Process can tap into the indivisible zero—that nothingness from which everything we desire is born. Indivisible, with liberty and justice for all. Everyone.

I remember a time before I discovered the Remembering Process, when my life felt lacking and my creative gears were jammed. As I write this to you now, I'm in a profound state of bliss: My wife has just given birth to our first child. This—coupled with the fact that I'm happy at work with a band I love, I find great joy in coaching musicians, I've finished my first book (see?), and I even got that perfect walkway built in my home (with the Ping-Pong table just where I remembered it)—tells me that the Remembering Process works. I'm living my best life and having a great deal of fun finding out what's around the next bend.

I remember that today was the start of a wonderful new chapter for you, too, as you live your best life.

You are already on the path. Keep growing.

AFTERWORD

by Joe Vitale

"You have to take seriously the notion that understanding the universe is your responsibility, because the only understanding of the universe that will be useful to you is your own understanding."

— Terence McKenna

Whenever I set an intention, invisible forces go to work. Earlier I told you that when I wanted to get back in shape, a friend of mine told me to check out a leading-edge, high-tech piece of fitness equipment called Nexersys —a computer game with standing pads that you punch and kick. I liked the idea of it and got the machine. Within weeks, I was getting trimmer and having a blast. But it got better.

I then downloaded the Nexersys app from iTunes. It's a game where, instead of striking a pad, you tap buttons as they appear on your screen. Imagine my surprise when the first lines were: "I am you from the future. If you want to get in shape like me, you need to train hard!"

Me from the future? I love this!

Let me give you one more example of how all this works: After recording four music albums in less than two years, I felt dead when it came to music. The creative flow dried up, and I had no more songs. No more passion or interest. I wanted to quit. Daniel and I discussed my feelings and of course turned to the Remembering Process. I went off into the future—mentally—and saw myself with another album completed. I couldn't see that happening from my present feelings, but I let it be. I didn't judge it.

I then decided to just go with it. I told Daniel that I would somehow write and record five more songs by that Christmas, which was only two months away. He playfully challenged me and raised the bar by saying, "Why not go for ten songs?"

Remember, I had *no* songs and *no* interest . . . but I allowed the process to unfold.

And get this: The very next day I had a new song. Then new ones came, about a dozen in all. I took them all, polished them, and was astonished by what I was receiving. When we went into the studio to record all ten tracks, the music was stunning. The soft songs were kissed by angels, and the rock songs raised the dead.

I'm still in awe of the fact that this music came from remembering it. After all, I had no musical inspiration before I spent a moment remembering the future. But once I allowed and accepted, the world opened up and treasures awaited me.

144

Your future self is waiting for you, too, and like the app I just described, all you have to do is "tap" that part of you. If you've been looking for something that can make your path easier, the Remembering Process is the way to do it.

And I guarantee that, from my experience, it's a whole lot of fun! But I'm sure you remember that, too.

As you go about your life for the next couple of weeks, intentionally look for places to use the Remembering Process. It will become second nature soon enough, but for now, stop yourself whenever you're feeling a little stuck, unsure, or uninspired and ask: *How can I use the Remembering Process to get me through this?*

Be ready to take the leap, to open your mind further than you expected to. Your mind holds infinite power and can take you wherever you dream.

I remember that you closed this book with a sense of curiosity and optimism, and I remember that it wasn't long before you had a creative breakthrough that had a major positive impact on the rest of your life. I remember feeling thankful that I had a part in it.

Thank you for picking up our book. I'm excited to see where you'll go with it.

THE REMEMBERING PROCESS IN ACTION

You don't have to take our word for it that the Remembering Process works. We've taught it to many of our clients and friends and have heard over and over how well it's worked for them, too. Here are some of their stories:

For me, remembering was a way to project myself metaphysically into the future. To remember implied the successful accomplishment of a goal. It takes pressure away from the mind-set that can trip up so many. "How we get there" becomes a mind-set of "how we got there." I think it made me work with a calm confidence toward my goals. Knowing that I already achieved my goal somewhere in time makes it so that you see your progress in a different perspective. You can relax knowing that your work will produce your desired outcome and actually enjoy the small progressions with the big ones because they represent the journey that got you to your goal. The journey is life, and we often don't stop to enjoy the process while in it. We usually just look back when it's over and only appreciate it then.

The Remembering Process brings you to the now. Creativity and inspiration come when you are in your calmest or quietest state. Playing with your psyche in this way allows you to bend traditional rules of thought to produce the outcome you want in reality. This reality-bending process is a steward for success with any goal. Although this is only one component of my success during this last year, it was an important working part of it.

— **Brandon Sparks** of the band Patton Sparks
(www.pattonsparks.com)
and Barton Creek Lending Group

I consider my proficiency at using the "remembering" tool to be novice at best. It has helped me in a few ways, but the common thread is this: It helps me see what I am truly capable of. I never remember anything that is outside the realm of possibility for me. That alone is where the true power is. There's a tremendous difference between hoping and wishing for an outcome versus really being self-confident and knowing you can do it without any hesitation. My brain allows only for realistic memories, so by remembering forward I open my eyes to my real potential. I would expect that outcome isn't unique to just me. The fact that the memories are actually realistic makes this concept invaluable.

In terms of my relationships, I've remembered my way out of insecurity, overexuberance, and nervousness. I've remembered forward about how strong and special I am in order to find my center and rise up in stressful situations. I've remembered my way into my true potential as a person who views love as a verb. Remembering forward helps me love better. It helps me visualize and wake up to my true potential output.

In terms of my work as a coach and sensei, re-membering forward has helped my students open their eyes to their own potential. I start small with them . . . remembering doesn't have to be about the most grandiose of goals. For those who want to get in excellent shape, I tell them, "You cannot out-train a bad diet." Instead of focusing on a memory of that perfect beach-ready body, I focus them on a memory of their breakfast tomorrow morning. Sim-ply that—I remember for them, saying things like, "I remember you waking up and thinking, *Today's the day I get on that horse and stop with the b.s. excuses.* I remember you had a half-cup of oatmeal and three egg whites. I remember you thought to yourself, *Wow, this isn't actually hard to prepare.* I remember you feeling better, cleaner, and more energetic as a result. I remember you realizing that you could be a doer and not just a talker."

For a more long-term goal like getting a brown belt, I introduce blue-belt students to the concept as follows: "I remember that day in the grappling class where you tapped out everyone on the mat.

Even those twice your size and just as experienced . . . do you remember that?" By posing that question and giving them that scenario or memory, I've just given purpose and direction to the disciplined repetition of triangle chokes or arm locks. I'll go on to say, "I also remember you went to the beach that weekend right after your promotion to brown belt . . . you took off your shirt and everyone you were with said, 'Oh, my God, what the hell do you do? I've never seen someone in that kind of shape.' Remember that? I remember your kickboxing was at a new level . . . offense, defense, conditioning, movement—all coming together at a true elite level. Remember?"

I can see it go off in their head. They do see it and remember. They see the best version of themselves that they can be. And it's not some fantasy— they realize that they can actually do it.

— **Sean Nolan,** martial artist

The Remembering Process is like a "strengthening of the mind" exercise, but it runs so much deeper than an exercise. It is actually a reality. When I truly let down my guard and allowed my thoughts to feel what it would mean—what the sounds would be, what the air smelled like, the temperature of the room, the other people who were there with me at the moment of success—what I wanted was no longer a hope, a dream, a goal, or an assertion. It was reality. Because I really and deeply felt like it had already happened. I allowed myself to go so deeply into that moment that tears came to my eyes. At the same moment a calming came over me that I'd never felt before, and it has stayed. The stress of getting to that moment, the longing and feelings of frustration that success seemed so far away, disappeared. Remembering made me not only visualize what I wanted, but it has also made me believe that I've already been there. Skepticism, fear of failure, fear of success—I've been through it all; and when I feel those things creep up, I go back to remembering.

— **Josh Patton** of the band Patton Sparks
www.pattonsparks.com

Remembering and creativity have long been co-creators of our stories, songs, movies, novels, innovations, dreams, relationships, and all things human. Recognizing this essential connection is such an act of genius. It has been right there in front of us forever. I first heard about the Remembering Process through conversing with Dan Barrett, and I'm so thankful to Dan and Joe for recognizing its value and bringing this book to fruition. It fascinated me, and I decided to immediately put it into practice with my music students. In no time, students in my songwriting classes were working through blocks with ease and attaining the authentic results we both wanted.

In applying this practice to instrumentalists, I quickly found that looking to the future to define the present was a remarkable shortcut to accomplishing previously unimagined songs and skills. I've used it to help mentor artists by asking them to imagine themselves wildly succeeding at their endeavors. What do they look like? How do they feel? What is different compared to the present moment? What skills do they need to master to get there? This process is helping to define self-creation and offers hope, growth, and, above all, possibility.

Finally, I tried using the Remembering Process in my own songwriting, and my first attempt yielded what I feel to be my most satisfying and complete song yet. I can imagine this book helping many people to create a better world for us all!

— **Kevin Carroll,** music edUKEcator
www.kevincarroll.net

As a love and relationship coach and counselor, I am constantly encouraging couples to "dream into" the life they desire as individuals in a partnership. The Remembering Process offers people who are committed to creating a loving space together a concrete road map to follow in a landscape that can sometimes feel confusing and full of surprise twists and turns. The notion of "belief mode" is a wonderful tool for couples who want to manifest a beautiful, nurturing space where they support one another in a shared vision.

— **Jeffrey Sumber,** relationship coach and psychotherapist
www.jeffreysumber.com

The Remembering Process gave me courage to try new things. After all, isn't it easier to remember something that already happened than to come up with something new? Framing new experiences, dreams, and far-off desires by remembering them first made them seem more attainable and real, and lessened the anxiety I had about "how"—and changed the question to "when."

— **Heather Miller,** musician
www.heathermillermusic.com

I've used the Remembering Process to great effect in my life as a musician in both the creative and business aspects of my process. On a day-to-day basis, it allows me to progress through a day full of tasks and small projects with a clearheaded approach and plan. As a performer, I'm able to re-member each performance as I want it to be, which helps me be open and grounded onstage because I have meditated on the outcome of the show. On a broader scale, this process is exceptionally help-ful for goal setting and achievement. The Remem-bering Process opens up pathways and possibilities for me in those times when I am stuck in a self-defeating cycle; it helps me see past my own nose and opens up my world.

— **Jana Pochop,** singer, songwriter, and content creator
www.janapochop.com

LINKS AND RESOURCES

Dr. Joe Vitale: www.mrfire.com

Daniel Barrett: www.rubiconartistdevelopment.com

Gay Hendricks, Ph.D., describes "Einstein Time" in his book *The Big Leap*: www.thebigleap.net. More of his wisdom and teachings can be found at www.hendricks.com.

Win Wenger, Ph.D., creator of Image Streaming: www.winwenger.com

Fred Alan Wolf, physicist and one of Joe's co-stars in the movie *The Secret*. If you'd like to learn more about quantum time, check out his work: www.fredalanwolf.com.

The Long Now Foundation was established in 1996 to creatively foster long-term thinking and responsibility in the framework of the next 10,000 years: www.longnow.org.

Great interviews and resources about the cosmos, consciousness, and God can be found at www.closertotruth.com.

Future Letter: www.futureme.org

Miracles Coaching: www.MiraclesCoaching.com

BIBLIOGRAPHY

Allen, James. *As A Man Thinketh.* Boston: Thomas Y. Crowell, 1913.

Arntz, William; Chasse, Betsy; and Vicente, Mark. *What the Bleep Do We Know? Discovering the Endless Possibilities for Altering Your Everyday Reality.* Deerfield Beach, FL: Health Communications, 2005.

Atkinson, William Walker. *Thought Vibration, or The Law of Attraction in the Thought World.* Chicago: New Thought Publishing, 1906.

Atwater, P.M.H. *Future Memory.* Charlottesville, VA: Hampton Roads, 1999, 2013.

Braden, Gregg. *The Divine Matrix: Bridging Time, Space, Miracles, and Belief.* Carlsbad, CA: Hay House, 2007.

Bristol, Claude M. *The Magic of Believing.* New York: Pocket Books, 1991.

Byrne, Rhonda. *The Secret.* New York: Atria Books/Beyond Words, 2006.

Chandler, Steve. *Time Warrior: How to Defeat Procrastination, People-Pleasing, Self-Doubt, Over-Commitment, Broken Promises, and Chaos.* Anna Maria, FL: Maurice Bassett, 2011.

Coates, Denise. *Feel It Real! The Magical Power of Emotions.* DeniseCoates.com, 2006.

Davies, Paul. *About Time: Einstein's Unfinished Revolution.* New York: Touchstone, 1995.

Dyer, Dr. Wayne W. *The Power of Intention: Learning to Co-Create Your World Your Way.* Carlsbad, CA: Hay House, 2004.

Eker, T. Harv. *Secrets of the Millionaire Mind: Mastering the Inner Game of Wealth.* New York: HarperCollins, 2005.

Fengler, Fred, and Varnum, Todd. *Manifesting Your Heart's Desires.* Book I and Book II. Burlington, VT: HeartLight, 2002.

Ford, Debbie. *The Dark Side of the Light Chasers.* New York: Riverhead Books, 1998.

Garnier-Malet, Lucille and Jean-Pierre. *Change Your Future Through Time Openings.* 2011.

Goddard, Neville. *Immortal Man: A Compilation of Lectures.* Camarillo, CA: DeVorss & Company, 1984.

Gott, J. Richard. *Time Travel in Einstein's Universe: The Physical Possibilities of Travel Through Time.* New York: Mariner Books, 2002.

Grabhorn, Lynn. *Excuse Me, Your Life Is Waiting: The Astonishing Power of Feelings.* Charlottesville, VA: Hampton Roads, 2003.

Hartong, Leo. *Awakening to the Dream: The Gift of Lucid Living.* Salisbury, United Kingdom: Non-Duality Press, 2001.

Hawkins, David R., M.D., Ph.D., *Power vs. Force: The Hidden Determinants of Human Behavior.* Carlsbad, CA: Hay House, 2002.

Hicks, Esther and Jerry (the Teachings of Abraham®). *Ask and It Is Given: Learning to Manifest Your Desires.* Carlsbad, CA: Hay House, 2004.

Katie, Byron; with Stephen Mitchell. *Loving What Is: Four Questions That Can Change Your Life.* New York: Three Rivers Press, 2002.

Landrum, Gene N., Ph.D. *The Superman Syndrome: The Magic of Myth in the Pursuit of Power: The Positive Mental Moxie of Myth for Personal Growth.* iUniverse, 2005.

Lapin, Jackie. *The Art of Conscious Creation.* Charleston, SC: Elevate, 2007.

Lederman, Leon M., and Hill, Christopher T. *Quantum Physics for Poets.* New York: Prometheus Books, 2011.

Lipton, Bruce H., Ph.D., *The Biology of Belief: Unleashing the Power of Consciousness, Matter & Miracles.* Carlsbad, CA: Hay House, 2008.

Lynch, David. *Catching the Big Fish: Meditation, Consciousness, and Creativity.* New York: Jeremy P. Tarcher/Penguin, 2006.

McTaggart, Lynne. *The Intention Experiment: Using Your Thoughts to Change Your Life and the World.* New York: Free Press, 2007.

Miller, Carolyn, Ph.D. *Creating Miracles: Understanding the Experience of Divine Intervention.* Tiburon, CA: H.J. Kramer, Inc., 1995.

Pickover, Clifford A. *Time: A Traveler's Guide.* New York: Oxford University Press, 1998.

Rhinehart, Luke. *The Book of est.* 2009. www.thebookofest.com.

Root-Bernstein, Robert and Michèle. *Sparks of Genius: The 13 Thinking Tools of the World's Most Creative People.* New York: Mariner Books, 1999.

Vitale, Joe. *The Attractor Factor: 5 Easy Steps for Creating Wealth (or Anything Else) from the Inside Out.* Hoboken, NJ: J. Wiley & Sons, 2008.

——. *Faith.* Toronto: BurmanBooks, 2013.

——. *The Miracles Manual: The Secret Coaching Sessions.* Hypnotic Marketing, Inc., 2013. www.miraclesmanual.com.

Wattles, Wallace D. *How to Get What You Want.* 1909.

——. *The Science of Getting Rich.* New York: Jeremy P. Tarcher/Penguin, 2007.

Wright, Kurt. *Breaking the Rules: Removing the Obstacles to Effortless High Performance.* Boise, ID: CPM, 1998.

ᛁᛁᛁᛁᛁ ACKNOWLEDGMENTS ᛁᛁᛁᛁ

Thank you to my beautiful wife, Andrea. This book would not exist without you and your encouragement. You turn me into somebody loved. Jana Pochop (janapochop .com), I appreciate you so much. You make life, business, and art flow for me. You are integral to all of my work. Thank you. Mathes Sclafani: Thank you for loving these words. Love is a verb! Thanks to C.J. Johnson for sparking the relationship with Joe, and for introducing me to life-changing audio books. Thank you to Natalie Goldberg for keeping my pen moving for almost 20 years, if even from afar. The Rubicon artists and their families, you have given me so much to be grateful for. Let's continue to grow each other's dreams! Thank you to the Sumber family, the Wulwick family, Michelle Bohls, Doc, Kevin Carroll, the porterdavis family, Nerissa Oden, Mark Hallman, and Gay Hendricks.

I'd like to give a special thank-you to my co-author, time traveler, and exceptional friend, Joe. Someone who loves music, personal growth, friendship, and truth as much as you do is a rare thing. Someone who shows up and does something about it is even rarer. I am so grateful for your presence in my life, and to share this part of our journey together.

With love,
Dan, from the vast expanse of the great big "Now"

❂

Key people who helped bring this book into being are Suzanne Burns and Mathes Jones. Jenna Glatzer helped us expand and polish the book. Also thanks to Nerissa, my love, for her ongoing support while I do fun things like create music and write this book. Thanks to Arielle Ford for introducing me to Reid Tracy, the CEO and president of Hay House; and thanks to Mathew Dixon for "attracting for others" the goal of publication. And, of course, I lovingly thank Daniel for teaching me the Remembering Process and helping me bring my music to life by "remembering" it.

With love,
Joe, from wherever "I" am

☺ ☺ ☺

·ıı ı ı ı ABOUT THE AUTHORS ı ı ı ı ·

Daniel Barrett is an acclaimed producer, musician, coach, and devoted student of life. He grew up in New York and graduated with a degree in music from the University of Massachusetts under the mentorship of composer David Patterson.

After spending some years in the Northeast teaching, producing, and performing, he founded his band porterdavis (www.loveporterdavis.com) with percussionist Mike Meadows. The band cut its teeth performing in the subway every morning at Porter and Davis Squares in Boston for the 5 A.M. commuter crowd. The cold and rainy Boston weather soon wore thin, and porterdavis packed up their instruments and relocated to warm and sunny Austin, Texas, where the band built a fervent fan base and released their self-titled, critically acclaimed album in 2009.

Porterdavis recorded the album with legendary producer and one of Daniel's music heroes, Gurf Morlix. The album spent nine weeks on the Americana chart and, as one reviewer put it, it was "nuclear badass on a stick times 12."

Porterdavis toured internationally, won Best Roots Rock Band at the 2009 Austin Music Awards, and was a Kerrville Folk Festival "New Folk Finalist," where the band performed on the Kerrville main stage. The band has shared the stage with Melissa Etheridge, The Neville Brothers, Brad Delp of the band Boston, The Subdudes, and others.

Daniel is also the founder and CEO of Rubicon Artist Development (www.rubiconartistdevelopment.com). In this game-changing and innovative music studio and development program, he mentors artists of all styles and levels.

In addition, he continues to practice his lifelong passion of production, and has produced award-winning artists Nate Borofsky (the Boston Music Award–winning album *Never Enough Time*), Patton Sparks (www.pattonsparks .com), and many others.

He also serves as musical producer and advisor to Dr. Joe Vitale.

From studying music in Ghana, West Africa, to graduating from the National Outdoor Leadership School (NOLS), to being a marathon runner and an Iyengar yoga practitioner, Daniel lives each day as a student of life, rhythm, and energy, and as an advocate for full expression and radical possibility.

He lives in Austin with his wife, Andrea; their son, Henry Wolf; and canine daughter, Tupelo Honey.

Website: www.DanielBarrettMusic.com

Dr. Joe "Mr. Fire!" Vitale is the author of way too many books to mention, including the bestsellers *The Attractor Factor, Life's Missing Instruction Manual,* and many more, from the head spinner *Zero Limits* to the mega-hit *The Key*. His recent book *Attract Money Now* is free at www.attractmoneynow.com. He's also recorded numerous best-selling audio programs, including *The Power of Outrageous Marketing, The Missing Secret,* and *The Secret to Attracting Money.*

Joe is a star in the movies *The Secret, The Opus, The Compass, The Tapping Solution, Leap!, Beyond Belief, The Meta Secret,* and *Openings.* He's been a popular guest on television numerous times since the late 1990s, from local shows to *Larry King Live.* He's been on ABC, CNN, PBS, and many more networks.

Of course, he's now a musician and has released the following albums: *Blue Healer, Strut!, Aligning to Zero* and *At Zero* (with Mathew Dixon), *The Healing Song,* and *Sun Will Rise.*

The creator of Miracles Coaching, Hypnotic Writing, Hypnotic Marketing, and The Awakening Course, Joe lives outside of Austin, Texas, with his wife, Nerissa, and their critters. His main website is www.JoeVitale.com.

Hay House Titles of Related Interest

YOU CAN HEAL YOUR LIFE, the movie,
starring Louise Hay & Friends
(available as a 1-DVD program and an expanded 2-DVD set)
Watch the trailer at: www.LouiseHayMovie.com

THE SHIFT, the movie,
starring Dr. Wayne W. Dyer
(available as a 1-DVD program and an expanded 2-DVD set)
Watch the trailer at: www.DyerMovie.com

THE BIOLOGY OF BELIEF: Unleashing the Power of Consciousness, Matter & Miracles, by Bruce H. Lipton, Ph.D.

E²: Nine Do-It-Yourself Energy Experiments That Prove Your Thoughts Create Your Reality, by Pam Grout

MANIFEST YOUR DESIRES: 365 Ways to Make Your Dreams a Reality, by Esther and Jerry Hicks (the Teachings of Abraham®)

THE MOSES CODE: The Most Powerful Manifestation Tool in the History of the World, by James F. Twyman

TUNE IN: Let Your Intuition Guide You to Fulfillment and Flow, by Sonia Choquette

WISHES FULFILLED: Mastering the Art of Manifesting, by Dr. Wayne W. Dyer

All of the above are available at your local bookstore,
or may be ordered by contacting Hay House (see next page).

We hope you enjoyed this Hay House book. If you'd like to receive our online catalog featuring additional information on Hay House books and products, or if you'd like to find out more about the Hay Foundation, please contact:

Hay House, Inc., P.O. Box 5100, Carlsbad, CA 92018-5100
(760) 431-7695 or (800) 654-5126
(760) 431-6948 (fax) or (800) 650-5115 (fax)
www.hayhouse.com® • www.hayfoundation.org

Published and distributed in Australia by: Hay House Australia Pty. Ltd., 18/36 Ralph St., Alexandria NSW 2015 • *Phone:* 612-9669-4299 *Fax:* 612-9669-4144 • www.hayhouse.com.au

Published and distributed in the United Kingdom by: Hay House UK, Ltd., Astley House, 33 Notting Hill Gate, London W11 3JQ • *Phone:* 44-20-3675-2450 • *Fax:* 44-20-3675-2451 • www.hayhouse.co.uk

Published and distributed in the Republic of South Africa by: Hay House SA (Pty), Ltd., P.O. Box 990, Witkoppen 2068 • *Phone/Fax:* 27-11-467-8904 • www.hayhouse.co.za

Published in India by: Hay House Publishers India, Muskaan Complex, Plot No. 3, B-2, Vasant Kunj, New Delhi 110 070 *Phone:* 91-11-4176-1620 • *Fax:* 91-11-4176-1630 • www.hayhouse.co.in

Distributed in Canada by: Raincoast Books, 2440 Viking Way, Richmond, B.C. V6V 1N2 • *Phone:* 1-800-663-5714 • *Fax:* 1-800-565-3770 www.raincoast.com

Take Your Soul on a Vacation

Visit www.HealYourLife.com® to regroup, recharge, and reconnect with your own magnificence. Featuring blogs, mind-body-spirit news, and life-changing wisdom from Louise Hay and friends.

Visit www.HealYourLife.com today!